SECRETS OF THE CCP'S UNITED FRONT WORK DEPARTMENT

SECRETS OF THE CCP'S UNITED FRONT WORK DEPARTMENT

MEMOIR OF A UNITED FRONT CADRE

CHENG GANYUAN

Translated from Chinese by Phoenix

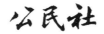

CITIZEN PRESS

Washington, D.C., United States

Initiatives for China, headquartered in Washington, DC, is a non-profit organization and grassroots movement dedicated to advancing a peaceful transition to democracy in China.

www.citizenpress.com

Translation and cover design by Phoenix

Issued by YANG Jianli

ISBN: 978-1-950834-21-1 (Print)

ISBN: 978-1-950834-22-8 (ebook)

Printed in the United States of America

Contents

Introduction

I am now nearly 80 years old. According to the traditional Chinese saying, it's a rarity to live to 70. Although advancements in medicine and living conditions have increased human life expectancy to beyond 70 or even 80, at this age a person's lifetime is nearing its end. Eighty years is but a brief moment in the history of mankind; yet concerning an individual's journey of life, it is already the diminishing light of a setting sun.

Most people at this age are already retired and have the means to free themselves from the daily grind and enjoy a world of tranquility beyond the world's turmoil. According to the well-known verse, *"The setting sun is infinitely endearing, but the light of day is disappearing."* The scene before sunset is indeed beautiful and magnificent. If we could free ourselves from dwelling on the approaching end, we could truly appreciate the universe's vastness and magnificence and experience a bliss that transcends time and space.

For those healthy and intellectually active, 80 is only midway through their senior years. They may yet have ten or twenty more years to fulfill their aspirations and engage in tasks that please them.

Older people like to reminisce about the past. After a long and eventful life, they now have plenty of time to indulge in the recollection of memories. I believe that every senior's deeply cherished memories of personal experiences are of value to mankind.

Perhaps as a result of the Creator's arrangement, our individual fates differ greatly. Some lead an undistinguished life that is nevertheless peaceful and contented. Some stand out among peers and acquire great wealth and high positions or earn eternal glory in history. Others suffer great misfortunes and lead a life of misery. Together all of these lives weave the colorful tapestry of a nation's fate. This is true history. If every person of advanced age were to write down his or her personal chronicles, this would be the most authentic record of the country's history and would enable our offspring to truly understand and cherish the past. Truthful historical narratives are highly valuable to a country's development.

Over the past several years, a profusion of so-called "memoirs" of famous people has appeared in China. Most of these authors are driven by economic interests and intend to profit from sensationalizing their lives. Among them, there are three main types: First, self-revealing memoirs by famous performance artists (movie stars, singers, talk show hosts, etc.) catering to their fans. A newly debuted star in her twenties or thirties may write extensively about how she worked hard until becoming famous overnight and about the romantic relationships she has been involved in. The author crisscrosses the country promoting her book, which may sell several hundred thousand copies and enchant many young fans, bringing the author both fame and fortune. This kind of promotion is most appealing to the media, who eagerly act in concert to spread the news. A famous talk show host may use his fame to self-promote his memoir, painting himself as a righteous man and a role model for young people aspiring to become famous. Not long after, the media may report some shameful secrets of the author, leaving readers feeling cheated. No wonder some in the Chinese publishing industry have called for a campaign to fight fabrications in memoirs.

Then there are memoirs which are published with the aid of political power. This type of memoir is even more shameless than the previous one. The authors are current or former high-level officials whose desire for fame and fortune is insatiable. Some hire a ghostwriter to blatantly laud their achievements. Some are managed by their children, who take advantage of their residue influence to deceive the readers. This method of reincarnation in another disguise is political betrayal and a polluting of Chinese history studies. Some utilize public resources to publish a memoir for political purposes and private profit. No wonder the following limerick circulates among common people in China: *"Local officials at 59, central officials at 69, not retiring until enough money is raked in; ending with a memoir, leaving with a million-dollar royalty."* Such officially published memoirs, rather than glorifying the authors, leave behind a political laughingstock.

Thirdly, there are memoirs as records of actual events, which are popular among common readers and hated by those in power or even banned by the government. These memoirs are mainly truthful reflections on historical events in mainland China based on the authors' personal experiences, which help to convey a true depiction of history. They remind people that history should not be distorted or forgotten. Prominent examples include Zhang Yihe's lengthy memoirs **Past Events are Not like Smoke** about the Anti-Rightist

Campaign and ***Past Events of Performance Artists***, which the General Administration of Press and Publication of China attempted to ban. These memoirs are of great intellectual depth and historical value. Through the bitter experiences of intellectuals known to the author personally, readers can come to an understanding of the miserable lives of upright intellectuals under Mao's nearly 30 years of rule. These books are popular among the common people because of their authenticity, which indicates that people desire true historical accounts and reject obvious fabrications. Because of the shock waves they produce in society, these books are destined to be disliked by those in power who stubbornly try to maintain the present despotic order. However, despite the many means with which authorities attempt to suppress these books, they will forever be treasured by the people. The fact that they continue to sell for high prices on the black market clearly demonstrates that justice resides in the hearts of the people.

From the above analysis, it is obvious that in order to write a memoir that is valuable to society, the author must satisfy the following three conditions:

First, the author must possess free will, that is, freedom of thought not controlled or bound by external factors. Independent thought is only possible in the absence of external control, suppression, or fear. In mainland China there is a state-sponsored Writer's Society. After becoming high-ranking members of the Writer's Society, a number of writers who had become famous before the communist takeover stopped producing any work of intellectual depth and only echoed official propaganda. This indicates that there exists no free expression without independence of personality and that freedom of thought is the fundamental essence of mankind.

Only a person with free will can regard the past without bias and face squarely the present and the future. In the words of the Russian poet Alexander Pushkin: *"Free element, o Sea!"* Life originated from the sea, and the sea represents all the original drivers of mankind's freedom. Mankind has only been able to achieve its splendid present conditions by innovating and developing freely. Free human thought is the basis of all cultural advancements, whether in terms of spirituality, material wealth, or social progress. A nation which restricts the expression of free will is unable to compete among other nations of the world.

Montesquieu, the great French political thinker of the Enlightenment period, argued in *The Spirit of the Laws* that a despotic regime maintained its rule based on the people's fear, whereas a democracy relied on the people's free will. During my over 50 years living in communist China, I lived constantly under the fear of external suppression by force and struggled unceasingly to exercise my free will. One political movement came after another, and countless intellectuals lost their lives attempting to exercise free expression. With everyone afraid to speak their mind, the result was a society based on lies. Eventually no one feels shame about lying, and everyone learns to echo the propaganda while knowing one is speaking against one's own convictions. Once lying becomes habitual, no one knows any longer what is true and what is false, what is glorious and what is shameful, apart from declarations coming from the supreme leader. If your opinions are not in lockstep with the Party line, you are immediately condemned as among the "shameful." Is it not a tragedy of grand proportions that the people of a nation with five thousand years of civilization are forced to live this way?

Over the past several years, I have often struggled with an acute self-criticism that kept me up late into the night. On one hand, I had to submit to force and do what I didn't want to do; on the other hand, I hated those in power for their many crimes against humanity. This painful internal struggle often prevented me from falling asleep. I came to believe that the greatest pain a human could experience was the torment of one's own soul. The writer Lu Xun wrote in *Shouting* about the painful souls of Chinese intellectuals who were constrained by ancient traditions. However, he could never have anticipated that thirty years after his death, the "new China" that he longed for would use the cruelest means to silence those whose only wish was to give voice to the truth.

I consider myself very fortunate to be enjoying freedom in the US in my senior years. Although it came late in life, this freedom is nevertheless precious to me. I can think freely and examine history and my personal past without constraints or suppressions, so that, God willing, my life may bring some degree of hope and light to this world.

Second, the author's purpose in writing a memoir should be pure. That is to say, the fundamental purpose of writing a memoir should be to speak the truth and compile an authentic record of history. To

4

achieve this, the author must be selfless and free of greed, not regarding the memoir as a means of attaining personal fame or profit. Many memoirs by famous people in mainland China nowadays are very political and contain lies that consciously distort history. Such memoirs can have negative political consequences. When Liu Shaoqi was persecuted, he said with regret that "history is written by the people." Sadly, these words came too late. When he blatantly flattered Mao as the "leader of the people" at the Seventh National Congress of the Chinese Communist Party (CCP) in Yan'an, he did not yet understand that the people are the judges of history. If CCP leaders respected the people in the beginning, how could these same people become tragic sacrifices of the CCP's internal conflicts? History is objective and just, and lies written in ink will never conceal truth written in blood.

Of the many memoirs that are flooding the book market in mainland China, how many are of high quality and based on truth? The people have a method of evaluation, which is to compare. Comparing these memoirs to those that truthfully reflect history, it is easy to determine which are false. No matter how extravagant the claims ("a role model for students" or "a man who changed China"), once the masks come off, they all turn out to be political cheats hawking snake oil. I've named this memoir "Secrets of the CCP's United Front Work Department" because I want readers to learn of a CCP insider's account and have no doubts about the true colors of CCP leaders and officials.

Memoirs can be a tool to distort history. Hitler's memoir painted this devil incarnate as a genius leader. Memoirs can also reveal the truth, exposing the evildoers who harm mankind. The difference between the two is whether the author dares to face history objectively and speak truthfully. This is what I meant earlier when I said that the intentions in writing a memoir must be pure.

While this is easy enough to understand, it is hard to implement. One must transcend oneself and get free of self-constraining biases and any pursuit of fame or profit before one can objectively and fairly confront history. Many political figures and powerful celebrities attempt to monumentalize themselves in their memoirs and portray themselves as upright and noble, without any mention being made of their faults or transgressions. In reality, even the most faultless and praiseworthy individuals in this world are humans and not gods, and are as imperfect as human nature itself. In addition, humans are inevitably influenced by their social environment, and especially when one lives in a distorted and corrupt society, few can avoid corruption altogether.

Confucius said: "*At fifty, I knew the mandate of Heaven. ...At seventy, I could follow what my heart desired, without transgressing what was right.*" Due to improved living conditions, people can live longer today, with the result that many people at fifty are still behaving as if they were in their youth. However, if someone at seventy still doesn't know what God's mandate is, then he or she has lived a life of childishness. To "know the mandate of Heaven" is to discover the trend of history and to avoid doing things that oppose the trend.

The societal developments of mankind, like the motions of celestial bodies, are naturally proceeding based on the Creator's arrangement and are not following any philosophical model. Marx used materialism to design a heaven on earth but ended up bringing about something more resembling a hell. Meanwhile, the progress of mankind has been toward constitutional democracy as a return to rationality. A wave of constitutional democracy that symbolizes the progress of human civilization began in the West in the 18th century and has since spread across the entire world. As a result of religious, racial, cultural, and economic conflicts, the world has experienced an unending series of wars, revolutions, and coups. During the 20th century, mankind experienced the catastrophes of two devastating world wars and the "social transformation" experiments in the name of socialism. In the span of a hundred years, several hundred million lives were lost in these adventures. Rather than retreat, the forces of democratization advanced after each catastrophe. In the past century of world history—through revolutions and restorations, suppressions and liberations, aggression and resistance—the trend has always been in the same direction, toward constitutional democracy. In the long flow of human history, magnificent events and remarkable personalities have been like ocean spray that disappears in an instant.

If we rationally review Chinese history over the past century, it is obvious that, as an ancient empire, China has been struggling under a wave of constitutionalism. From the 1911 revolution to the mid-century Chinese Civil War, from the Cultural Revolution in the 1960s and 1970s to the economic reform afterwards, the Chinese people have paid an unprecedented price for years of social experimentation. Some speculate that this is God's punishment for China's corrupted ancient traditions. After the painful lessons of the past century, the Chinese people have begun to recognize the advantages of constitutional democracy and will gradually merge into the historical tide of world civilization.

We can say that China, after the dark night of the 20th century, is beginning to see the light of day. Some have referred to the present century as China's century. I think it is more accurate to say that the 21st century is the century of China's merging with the worldwide movement toward constitutional democracy. Once this is achieved, we can imagine that China will enter a glorious phase, and that mankind will experience a fusion of the East and the West. A splendid chapter of human history will be upon us.

Time has come for a truthful description of history, so that later generations will understand China's difficulties in its progress toward constitutional democracy and use this example as a reminder of the need to strive for a democratic society.

Finally, in order to write a good memoir, not only must one have honest intentions, but there must also exist a liberal social environment and healthy living conditions, which are lacking in China.

In a liberal social environment, the government would guarantee freedom of the press, which is paid lip service in communist China's constitution but unattainable by the Chinese people. If a memoir attracts the attention of the Ministry of State Security, even before publication the author will be at risk of search and seizure and possibly imprisonment. The despotic tradition is still at work in China today, and not only suspicious writing but even just a loose tongue can get a person into a lot of trouble. There is an ancient saying that "*there are golden houses in books; there are beautiful girls in books.*" The implication is that a man can obtain fortune and love by studying hard. I think "there are killers in books" should be appended to this saying. How many of the elderly living in mainland China would dare to risk imprisonment and severe persecution for the sake of leaving behind an honest historical account? For example, a Committee of Cultural and Historical Materials was formed at the Political Consultative Conference, made up of former prisoners of war who served in the KMT military and received special pardon

7

from the CCP regime. They were given an assignment by the United Front to write about historical events without political implications. But they had been traumatized by prison and understood what the CCP really wanted in their writings, so none of them dared to reveal the truth about the CCP's dirty political machinations in the past. They did nothing but scold the KMT and sing the high praises of the CCP in their memoirs. While it is true that "a wise man submits to fate," the fact is that the cultural and historical materials these former POWs left behind are of very little value.

A "relaxed living environment" implies that the basic needs of the elderly must be met, or as the ancients said, "*Elders are looked after properly.*" Obviously, this is a necessary precondition for the composing of memoirs. When the elderly have no income or pension and are always worried about their next meal (as in the case of retirees from some enterprises in China whose pensions were not paid several months in a row and whose medical expenses are not reimbursed), how can they be expected to recount their life's journey at leisure?

I rejoice that as a senior I was able to come to a country where one can speak and write freely. Perhaps God felt sympathy with my sufferings and wanted to give me a chance to write an eye-witness account of my life. I live in a quiet senior living facility called Manor, where there are many immigrants from "socialist states" like China and the former Soviet Union among over one hundred residents. Sometimes we joke that "real socialism is in capitalist states that Marx demonized" and that we are enjoying the welfare created by capitalism.

I lived in Mainland China for 64 years, where I might have been referred to as a "screw" of the Party machine, sweating and bleeding for the red regime. It turned out this "screw" didn't have the right "thread," in that I have always retained a part of my humanity. Eventually, I like to think that I became a kind of crowbar that could be used to smash this man-eating machine. There is a popular saying that "ants gnaw the bones" among Chinese factory workers. Now that I don't rely on the CCP regime for my livelihood, readers should not be surprised that a "small ant" like me is gnawing a big bone like the CCP machine. Perhaps this is the logical consequence of treating people like ants.

My life has been somewhat legendary. When I was young, I didn't fear death. I became so fanatically patriotic by the age of 15 that I enlisted in the CCP military and entered Korea under the banner of "Forever-Successful Maoism." I fought in the Korean War for two and half years and left dozens of dead comrades-in-arms behind. I was lucky to return alive and, like other Chinese veterans of the Korean War, was referred to as one of the "dearest people" by the media in mainland Chinese at the time. Over half a century later, when I came to realize that the outcome of our sacrifices was that the people of North Korea lived under the dictatorship of the most hated man in the world, I felt that I had somehow managed to survive one of the worst nightmares of the century. Every time I recall my comrades-in-arms who died in the war and were buried in the frozen earth of Korea, I experience a deep grief that doesn't become any more bearable with time.

I entered college via the "cadre transfer" program in the 1950s, and subsequently worked in government and Party institutions at central and local levels, including nearly years at the United Front Work Department (UFWD). During the Cultural Revolution, as a result of someone smearing a portrait of Mao on the flyleaf of my notebook, I was instantly labeled an acting counterrevolutionary, imprisoned for a year, and exile to a rural village in northern Jiangsu Province to perform hard labor. After the Cultural Revolution, I engaged in legal research, became a professor of law, and published books. Recalling my life journey, I have been through heaven and hell. Since the time span of my experiences is quite extensive, it is difficult to include everything in one book, and hence I'd like to write several memoirs addressing separate topics. Assuming that my life experiences can be truthfully reflected in writing, I hope to provide an eyewitness account of the recent history of China.

I don't believe it is necessary to adhere to a strictly chronological sequence of events. I will simply follow my heart and focus on significant aspects of the moments in history I have lived through. This will form a series of memoirs which I hope will bear witness to the China of my lifetime.

From September 1961 to December 1970, I worked at or was associated with the UFWD of the municipal CCP committee in a city in southern China. These nearly ten years were an important period of my life. I have been inspired by Ms. Zhang Yihe's books, including *Past Events are Not like Smoke*, in which she recalled the experiences of her parents, friends, and members of the art scene and academia during the Anti-Rightist Campaign and the Cultural Revolution. Those she described in her books were all targets of the CCP's United Front work. Their honors and humiliations, triumphs and defeats, happiness and sorrows under the communist regime resembled an elaborate play. They were performers on the stage, and there were many directors giving behind-the-scenes directions. Although manipulated by the CCP's UFWD, they could never know the inner workings of this mysterious institution because it operated behind a screen known as "state secrets." I was only a small cadre in this behind-the-scenes institution, but my position gave me insight into the manipulations and deceptions of these performances.

Nowadays, this elaborate stage play put on by the United Front is still being performed in mainland China, and even more performers are involved. Its scope has spread from mainland China to Taiwan and overseas. Although the specific directorship has gone through several generations of cadres, the general director, which is the CCP, has never lost interest in this play, and sometimes its supreme leader has personally functioned as a director. The non-CCP political actors and CCP officials in makeup have given their best performance because of the enticements of fame, money, and power. This play has been put on year after year. However, like tricks of magic, once the tricks are revealed, the audience loses interest in the show. Although the people of mainland China have already seen through the United Front's tricks, these tricks continue to entertain those in Taiwan, Hong Kong, Macao, and overseas who crave titles and profit. They are like sheep drawn to the enticingly decorated entrance of the slaughterhouse.

As a former insider who once had all the tricks up my sleeve, I must follow my conscience now and do all I can to ward off those on the path to the slaughterhouse.

Perhaps it is time for the Chinese people to construct a giant stage where shifty, behind-the-scenes directors are not pulling all the strings. On the giant stage of constitutional democracy, people will choose to no longer make a compact with the devil but rather with the better angels of their nature. The people have been engaged in a life-and-death struggle with the CCP for control of the stage and the repertoire before the curtain is lifted on the great era. When the moment arrives, the marvelous performance of constitutional

10

democracy will embody the expression of every Chinese citizen, without fear and in the spirit of joy and love.

For the sake of the millions of Chinese who have lost their lives or who have suffered immeasurably to ignite the torch of hope that will light up the future, I'd like to borrow the words of the Czech writer Julius Fučík's as this memoir's epigraph:

"People, I love you, be careful!"

Cheng Ganyuan

California, United States

June 2015

Chapter 1: Inside the CCP's Power Structure

In 1954, I entered Fudan University Law Department's undergraduate program directly from the military as a "cadre-transfer student." It was a four-year program. However, in the second half of 1957, I was diagnosed with tuberculosis and, following my doctor's advice, took a one-year leave of absence. I resumed school in 1958.

That summer, Shanghai municipal Chinese Communist Party (CCP) committee secretary Ke Qingshi, who was also Secretary of the CCP's Eastern China Bureau, decided to consolidate all social, administrative, and legal studies institutions in Shanghai. As a result of this decision, Fudan University Law Department merged with Eastern China University of Political Science and Law and a few other schools to form the Shanghai Academy of Social Sciences. Following Mao Zedong's directive that social studies extend beyond the campus and out to the workers and peasants, the academy implemented the so-called "Education via Confrontation, Denunciation, and Transformation" program. All law majors were sent to Nantong County, Jiangsu Province, for a "Remedial Lesson in Land Reform."

We performed physical labor and participated in the "Land Reform Task Force" for the "Remedial Lesson in Suppressing Counterrevolutionaries." Led by Zhou Aimin, director of Jiangsu Province's Department of Supervision, the task force arrested over 500 people who had "historical problems" dating to before the establishment of the CCP regime, including former mayors of townships, members of Landlord's Restitution Corps, landlords, and rich peasants. Among the arrested was Mr. Gu, president of the County People's Court and a veteran CCP member since the early phase of WWII, whose alleged crime was shielding family members who were landlords. Gu was arrested as an "alien element of the class" and put in prison for over ten years. His case was eventually redressed after the Cultural Revolution. The task force organized "People's Tribunals," conducted crash interrogations, and publicly tried and executed over one hundred people in three short months. As law majors, we also took part in the case management team, organized paperwork, and worked as court clerks. Some of the defendants were only accused by one or two villagers of "blood debts before liberation," accusations they denied. However, these defendants were rushed to conviction without any investigation for corroborating evidence. Most were executed by firing squad in the commune square at night. Some of the convicts continued shouting "Injustice!" until their dying breath. We seriously questioned this method of trial, but as students we had no say in trial procedures or the outcomes of these cases. We were no more than "onlookers at the execution of revolutionists" in Lu Xun's novels.

The so-called "Remedial Lesson" brought an onslaught of disasters to the people of Nantong County. As rumors had it, the reason for this crash course in Land Reform and Suppressing Counterrevolutionaries was that Nantong County had been a model county during the KMT's regime, and there had been a few assassinations of township and village cadres in 1958, leading to the CCP committee's decision to carry out a mass crackdown. The redressing of the case of Mr. Gu (the above-mentioned president of the County Court) indicated that this was a "leftist" campaign. Quite likely, this kind of local massacre was not an isolated event but rather common during the Land Reform and the Campaign to Suppress Counterrevolutionaries, as the bloodshed attracted little attention.

In the summer of 1959, among the first batch of graduates of the Shanghai Academy of Social Sciences, over forty of us with good grades and good political conduct were selected for placement in central government institutions in Beijing. Most of us were assigned to the Ministry of Public Security, the Supreme Court, the Supreme People's Procuratorate, and the Security Department of the Chinese Academy of Sciences. I was the only one assigned to the Ministry of Interior. One of these schoolmates was envied by the others because he was assigned to a position in a "top-level work unit," the Security Bureau of Zhongnanhai (where CCP leaders live and work). He worked in public safety before entering college, and now he was the admiration of everyone because he was able to see Chairman Mao every day. Actually, he proved to be the unluckiest of all of us, becoming a "gray-haired palace maid." As if imprisoned inside those red walls, he had no personal freedom to speak of. Any errands run outside Zhongnanhai lasting over one hour in duration required a formal approval of absence by his superior, and personal phone calls were strictly forbidden. Not until the 1980s was he transferred to the Supreme People's Procuratorate, where he served as the deputy director of the reception office and received deputy division-level compensation. You could say this man had dedicated his whole life to the supreme leader Chairman Mao. Later in life, as a retired cadre, he still wore his veteran cadre's tunic and was completely out of sync with his surroundings, resembling a retired royal guard from a past imperial era.

On September 10, 1959, full of curiosity and exhilaration, I took a north-bound train to Beijing, double-checking that I had with me my assignment paperwork, administrative and organizational letters of introduction, and residence and food rationing registration. The letters of introduction we carried with us only had on them P.O. boxes and no actual addresses, because the office addresses of central government institutions were kept secret. Only phone numbers were listed on the letters in case those dispatched to meet us at the train station somehow missed us. Everything went rather smoothly. As soon as I got off the train, I saw a human resources officer of the Ministry of Interior holding a banner with my name on it. Toting my simple luggage, I went to the ministry to report for duty.

The ministry promptly dispatched me to make preparations for the establishment of a Civil Affairs Cadre School in the Guang'anmen area of Beijing, under the direction of Mr. Yue, the school's CCP committee office director. Zhang Yibai, deputy minister of the Ministry of Interior and a veteran of the Yan'an era, served concurrently as president of the school. Mr. Li, deputy director general of the Personnel Bureau of the State Council, was transferred to serve full-time as vice president of the school. My job title was CCP committee office executive secretary and Communist Youth League (CYL) general branch secretary.

When I took office, preparations were underway for the grand ceremony of the 10th National Day, and the capital appeared especially prosperous. Tian'anmen Square was being cleaned day and night because the Ten Grand Construction Projects—including the Great Hall of the People and the Museum of Revolutionary History right beside the square—were at the final stage of construction. The grand ceremony on Oct. 1st was fast approaching and we rushed to organize young cadres and workers to participate in the National Day parade and receive Chairman Mao's review. Everyone was to wear a pair of blue trousers and a white shirt. Before daybreak on October 1, we assembled at 5 o'clock and walked over two hours to Chang'an Boulevard, outside of Tian'anmen Square, to line up. We stood on the street for another three hours until the parade started at 10 o'clock. Although the weather was chilly, all of us were understandably excited. Our processions were the closest to the review stand on Tian'anmen, and we clearly saw Mao Zedong standing with Khrushchev. Khrushchev took off his hat and waved it at the crowd, his bald head reflecting the sunlight. Mao Zedong was situated just above his giant portrait on the Tian'anmen rostrum, causing momentary confusion as to which was the real Mao. At night we returned to Tian'anmen Square to celebrate with college students. Firework displays continued until one in the morning. After returning to the dorm, we were exhausted and slept until 4 o'clock in the afternoon. The canteen only served two meals a day during the holidays and we were barely in time to catch the last meal of the day.

No sooner had people recovered from the excitement of the National Day when they had to brace for a political storm that swept through the central government institutions. As Peng Dehuai was denounced in the Lushan Conference, the central government institutions began denouncing "right-leaning opportunism" and people involved with the "Peng Dehuai Clique." The Ministry of Interior became a focus of this "anti-right-leaning" movement. Its administrative deputy minister, Wang Ziyi, was a veteran cadre in the "Gang of the Northwest" and, as a native of northern Shaanxi Province, was a comrade-in-arms of Liu Zhidan (founder of the Shaaxi-Gansu Soviet Zone) and served as director general of the Department of Civil Affairs in the Yan'an Regional Government. He had appointed a few veterans of the "Gang of the Northwest" to positions in the Ministry, such as Mr. Li, vice president of the Cadre School, and Mr. Yue, my immediate superior, who was also Liu Zhidan's son-in-law. To eliminate the "pernicious influence" of the "Gang of the Northwest," Wang Ziyi was chosen to be the first target of denunciation, and a slew of cadres who were members of the "Gang" were implicated.

In charge of this rectification campaign was the newly inaugurated minister of the Ministry of Interior, Qian Ying, who took over the office from Xie Juezai. A woman of extraordinary prowess, she was one of the "twenty-eight and a half Bolsheviks" of the Wang Ming Clique in Moscow. Her husband was executed by firing squad by the KMT regime at Yuhuatai, Nanjing, in the 1930s. She never

15

remarried and lived with her mother. Having learned from the fierce struggles within the CCP, she was ruthless in persecuting people. She took charge of the all-hands meeting of ministry cadres to confront and denounce Wang Ziyi, who was also subjected to denunciation sessions in smaller meetings, in the same way as a landlord during the Land Reform. A Red Army veteran from northern Shaanxi experienced with internal struggles of the CCP, Wang maintained his dignity and showed no fear or remorse. He responded to all accusations with the same formulated answer: "If I have committed those mistakes, I will correct them. If I have not, I will take your words to guard against them." After over two weeks of meetings of all CCP members and cadres, there was still no definitive result. On the contrary, Wang had won the sympathy of many Party members.

This was the first time I had seen a high-level official holding his ground in denunciation meetings, and it left a deep impression on me. Wang was later removed from office, demoted to the position of deputy factory manager of a steel plant in Taiyuan, Shanxi Province, and severely persecuted during the Cultural Revolution. He was in his seventies when his case was redressed and he became a member of the Political Consultative Conference (PCC) and died peacefully. His fate can be compared with that of Qian Ying, who was imprisoned during the Cultural Revolution and died a painful death in the hospital.

The "anti-right-leaning" movement victimized other "Gang of the Northwest" cadres in the Ministry of Interior. Among my superiors, Mr. Li, vice president of the Cadre School and former deputy director general of the Personnel Bureau of the State Council, was demoted from Administrative Rank 9 to Rank 11. Mr. Yue, CCP committee office director, was demoted from Administrative Rank 12 to Rank 13. Later they were both transferred out of the Ministry and appointed to deputy positions in lower-level organizations.

The rectification campaign was followed by the Third National Conference of Civil Affairs. The aim of this conference was to implement the Lushan Conference's "anti-right-leaning" policy and to reduce or eliminate the influence of "Wang Ziyi's right-leaning line" on the Ministry of Interior. The conference was attended by directors general and deputy directors general of each province's Department of Civil Affairs and directors general of departments and bureaus directly under the ministry, for a total of over two hundred officials.

One of the items on the agenda was to listen to the CCP Central Committee Chief of Staff Yang Shangkun's recorded verbal report about the Lushan Conference. The three-hour-long report was highly classified, and only officials of Rank 13 or above were allowed to listen to it. However, since the magnetic wire on which the report was recorded was kept in the classified archives of the Central People's Broadcasting Station as top secret, it was required that the ministry dispatch two cadres to assist the classified recording specialist in retrieving and playing the wire. As a low-level cadre, I was assigned to this mission along with the director of the Office of Classified Materials and had the opportunity to listen to the entire report. Yang Shangkun described Peng Dehuai as an old-school warlord whose world view had not been reformed and whose hostility toward Mao had historical roots. According to Yang, some members of the CCP Central Committee revealed that Peng privately opposed Mao's cult of personality. In one of the gatherings of high-level officials of the People's Liberation Army (PLA), reporters tried to pull Peng and Mao together for a photo shoot, and Peng impatiently said, "Dog heads, human heads, what's the point of shooting those heads?" This expression was interpreted as an insinuating remark about Mao. Peng allegedly said to members of a "military club" that Mao read too many ancient books and had learned too many of the persecution tactics of ancient emperors. These rumors were dragged up in the conference and incited Mao's fury. Another accusation was that when Peng visited the Soviet Union, Mikoyan said to him, "We united to get rid of Belial, and the CCP could use the same method to treat Stalinists." We can well imagine that this kind of talk upset and even frightened Mao. At the Lushan Conference, Chen Boda specifically "exposed" Peng, classifying him as an old-school warlord. Some of the old field marshals also came forward to denounce Peng. Chen Yi referred to Peng as "a hero of the past, culprit of the present." Lin Biao likened Peng to Wei Yan in *Romance of Three Kingdoms*, who had a "rebellious bone" on the back of his head. These attacks essentially raised Mao to the level of emperor. Any disrespectful words or conduct toward him would be punished by death.

At this civil affairs conference, Vice Premier Chen Yi, on behalf of the CCP Central Committee and the State Council, spoke for over three hours mainly to support the denunciation of Wang Ziyi and to emphasize the importance for Party members and high-level cadres of adhering to Party rules. He said that Wang Ziyi repeatedly advised Chairman Mao to organize a National Veteran's Association. Chen Yi asserted that Wang hoped to fight the Ministry of Defense for control of the national paramilitary through the proposed association.

This was the first time since joining the party that I witnessed the power struggles taking place within the CCP. What I observed was worlds apart from my naïve expectations of what went on in a central government institution.

As the entire country was following the course of this "anti-right-leaning" movement, a nationwide famine was starting to spread to the capital. The delusional "Great Leap Forward" had brought about a tragic national disaster. At the time, our canteen provided a daily ration of 450g of grain, mostly in the form of steamed corn bread, and some boiled cabbage. When the famine started, news came from my hometown in Anhui Province about people starving to death. We were doubtful in the beginning. Before long, however, one of my classmates, Mr. Lu, who worked in the Ministry of Public Security, told me that all six members of his extended family who were living in the countryside, including his wife and son, had died of hunger. He took a bereavement leave to go back to his hometown of Chaohu for the burials. Upon his return to Beijing, the Ministry of Public Security reported the situation to the leadership of the State Council. Premier Zhou Enlai took the matter seriously, asking the minister to request a written report from Lu. This report might have later become an important piece of evidence influencing the central government's decision to dispatch Li Baohua to Anhui to investigate Zeng Xisheng's negligent leadership during the famine. This fellow from my province, who is the sole survivor of his family, still lives in Beijing, has retired and remarried.

In November 1960, the Ministry of Interior underwent a reorganization of its leadership. The former minister, Qian Ying, was transferred to the CCP's Central Discipline Inspection Commission to serve as secretary. Zeng Shan (Zeng Qinghong's father) became the new minister. At the time Zeng Qinghong was in high school, often bicycling in and out of the side entrance to the Ministry's compound at West Huangchenggen. Their whole family lived in the innermost courtyard of the Ministry's compound. After Zeng Shan took office, he began internal investigations and reassignments of cadres. In the case of those directors general and other cadres with "historical problems," he conducted both internal and external investigations. External investigations required frequent trips to locations outside of Beijing, which posed quite a burden for the investigators. The nation was engulfed in the famine at the time. Food was hard to come by outside of Beijing, especially in Northeastern China, even if you had grain rationing coupons. With a letter of introduction from the Ministry of Interior, investigators stayed at high-level guest houses such as Liaoning Hotel, but were only provided with sorghum for food, without rice or wheat. Only cadres ranked 13 and above were supplied with refined grains. Naturally, cadres with families were reluctant to take such trips. I lived alone in the Ministry's dorm and was frequently sent on month-long trips to Northeast China. As a result of the strenuous work, lack of nutrition, and gastroenteritis, I developed edema, and even walking became a struggle. Later, a cousin of mine who worked in the navy obtained some soy beans to supplement my diet, and I slowly recovered.

To celebrate the Chinese New Year of 1961, the Ministry organized a party. As the secretary of the general branch of the CYL, I was dispatched to invite Ma Ji from Central Broadcasting Troupe for a crosstalk performance. He and I were of similar age. At the time his organizational affiliation was still with Xinhua Bookstore and he had newly transferred to the Central People's Broadcasting Station on a temporary basis. After his performance, it was already after 10 pm. The cooks from the canteen made him a bowl of noodles, topped with a few thin pork strips and lots of cabbage. He quickly devoured the whole bowl and claimed that he hadn't had such delicious noodles in a long while. When he was done, he used a handkerchief to wrap up two veggie-and-meat buns given by the canteen to take home to his family. In comparison, today's performers are used to delicacies in their everyday meals and earn over a million RMB for an appearance. Who today could imagine the joy of a simple bowl of noodles in exchange for a performance?

In the spring of 1961, I traveled to the South to visit family and saw that the supply of food in Nanjing was slightly better than in Beijing. I also realized that my parents were getting old and needed help taking care of my daughter. More importantly, I was sick of the political climate of class struggle in the Ministry of Interior. I made the decision to request to be transferred to Nanjing. At that time, the

Cadre School was closed per decision from above. All personnel returned to the Ministry for new assignments from the Ministry's Bureau of Personnel. I grasped this opportunity to request the transfer. My superiors tried to persuade me to stay but finally yielded to my resolution. I completed the transfer in September and reported to the Nanjing municipal CCP Committee.

Chapter 2: Transferring to a Mysterious Office

In September 1961, I took along my letter of introduction to report to the Organization Department of the Nanjing municipal CCP committee. I was met by a deputy director in charge of cadre transfer and assignment who first said that because of the Party's trust in me, it was decided that I would be assigned to the United Front Work Department (UFWD). She went on to elaborate that the UFWD was a very important institution in the CCP committee, where cadres were held to high standards and had to have adequate levels of policy expertise plus a very strict sense of organizational discipline. Since I had been cultivated by the Party for many years and had stood stringent tests (probably related to my service in the military), the CCP committee decided, after careful consideration, to assign me to the UFWD. I was asked if I had any personal thoughts on the assignment. At the time I didn't have any special demands and thought any job would be fine as long as it was in an urban area not far from home. I accepted the assignment and promised to do my best.

The next morning, I took the bus and then walked for less than ten minutes to a compound on Hanfu Street at the eastern end of Changjiang Road. From the outside, it didn't look like a Party institution. The gate was very small and barely wider than a car, and remained closed unless a car needed to pass through, just as that of a private mansion. Pedestrians entered through a small door in the gate. There was a small doorkeeper's room inside with a phone to communicate with the offices. The inner yard contained a small garden with assorted young trees and some recently planted green vegetables, probably grown by the cadres for self-consumption. Behind the vegetable garden was a very elegant two-story building surrounded by tall cedars. The building was made of granite and had a basement. I entered the building through its side entrance as the main entrance was closed. To the right was a small auxiliary building where the kitchen and servant dorms were located, with a staircase reaching the second story of the main building directly. South of the main building was a rear garden that was formerly the front yard, containing a water fountain and a concrete bomb shelter, suggesting that the former owner of this building was no ordinary person.

This building had the appearance of an old German castle. Its second story had bedrooms with circular windows on two sides and a balcony, and its first level had an enormous living room and three smaller rooms. However, the roof was made of blue glazed tiles with flying beams in the style of a traditional Chinese temple. Judging from its exterior, this building was at most a little over ten years old and was probably constructed after China's victory in WWII. Its location at the intersection of Hanfu Street and Changjiang Road further indicated its former owner's high status. The older generation in Nanjing all knew that Changjiang Road was formerly named National Government Road. From this building, walking along the road for about four or five hundred meters, you would reach the Republic of China's highest government office, the Presidential Palace. Continuing one more block, you would come upon the National Great Hall, where the National Constituent Assembly and the first National Assembly, which elected the president of the Republic of China, convened. To the north of this building along Hanfu Street was the famous New Meiyuan Village, where Zhou Mansion (the office and residence of the former CCP Delegation to Nanjing, including such high officials as Zhou Enlai, Dong Biwu, and Li Weihan) was located. Surrounding the CCP Delegation Office in New Meiyuan Village were some small two-story buildings like those in alleyways in Shanghai, much smaller than the mansion on Hanfu Street that became the UFWD office building. After the communist takeover, Zhou Mansion became the CCP Delegation History Museum. According to exhibits in this museum, all the buildings around Zhou Mansion were rented or bought by the KMT intelligence agency, whose spies monitored all activities in the mansion.

Anyone who could afford such an elegant residence located at such a politically sensitive location must have had extraordinary social status and political background. I later learned that its former owner was a major-general of the KMT air force who came from a prominent family. He fled to Taiwan shortly before the communist takeover, and the property was confiscated by the CCP.

It is ironic that many of the buildings around Hanfu Street were formerly the KMT's base to monitor the CCP Delegation Office and CCP members' activities. What a difference a few short years can make! The building that I entered was still used for special political monitoring, but the roles had been reversed, and this building had become the CCP's base to monitor intellectuals (in minor political parties) and former KMT political and military officials who stayed behind on the mainland after the KMT government fled. At this point, I can't help recalling the verse by Li Yu, the last ruler of the Southern Tang Empire: *"Last night, in the attic revisited by the eastern wind, it was unbearable to look toward home in the fair moonlight."* Now, over a thousand years later, the Chinese people were forced to endure nearly a hundred years of political storms, witness a series of regime changes and suffer untold casualties.

I entered this mysterious institution and its aura of secrecy, and was greeted by a deputy director of its Personnel Division named Zhang, who was apparently a military veteran, still wearing an old military uniform that was washed of all color. He introduced himself by saying that he was formerly the deputy commissar of a military regiment and felt a certain rapport with me since I had also served in the military. He briefly introduced the internal structure of the Nanjing municipal UFWD, which contained three divisions and one office: a Political Parties Division, a Business Sector Division, a Personnel Division, and the Department Office. The Department was staffed by a director general, Mr. Wang, who was concurrently a vice mayor of the municipality, and two deputes of him: Ms. Wang, who was the actual administrator; and Mr. Ma, who was in charge of ethnic and religious affairs. The total number of employees, including a typist, was only 23. It was an extremely lean and efficient institution.

To emphasize the importance of United Front work, Mr. Zhang explained that all its employees were required to be CCP members, because the Party's confidential information was involved in United Front work. The work must strictly adhere to confidentiality rules and could not be carried out by outsiders. When he mentioned the UFWD's particular functions, due to the fact that this deputy director grew up in a working-class family and had a very limited knowledge base, he couldn't explain it clearly. Nevertheless, because of his repeated emphasis on the policy to "ally with, educate, and transform" minor political parties' members and figures without party affiliations, I began to have a vague notion. In the end, he handed me two printouts, one titled ***Mao Zedong on the United Front*** and the other a collection of documents from the CCP Central Committee's conferences on United Front work. He also asked me to read the internal periodicals about United Front work published by the UFWD of the Party Central.

Deputy Director Zhang then explained that the organization had decided to assign me to the Political Parties Division. As for the function of this division, he didn't explain much, apart from some generalizations about communicating with members of minor political parties and non-partisan figures. He told me I would learn the specifics from my senior colleagues.

I was led to the various offices to meet my senior colleagues individually. Deputy Director General Wang was introduced to me as a senior cadre whose career dated back to the CCP's guerrilla faction in Nantong Prefecture during WWII. She had already risen to become secretary of the prefecture CCP committee before the establishment of the CCP regime, and was later transferred to the municipality to serve as district CCP committee secretary before coming to the UFWD. She looked very much like a heroine and spoke open-heartedly with the heroic spirit of a revolutionary woman. She spoke to me as an elder sister would, saying, "You are young and well-educated at the university. Study hard and work hard, and you'll have a bright future. We are confident that you will become a new force in our department."

Next, I went to the Business Sector Division to meet its director and two officers. All three were former underground CCP members in Nanjing during the KMT era, and it so happened that the director led labor movements in a factory in Pukou Township, one of the officers was a leader in the student movement, and the other officer led the commerce sector's underground struggles when he worked at the Central Emporium. These were extraordinary capabilities covering three different domains. Finding myself in the presence of such highly competent individuals, I felt like a grammar school student out of place among university students.

Previously, I had only had superficial impressions of the nature of United Front work and believed this institution specialized in dealing with minor political parties. This impression came from my father's perspective as a member of a minor political party. My father was a scholar with a lifelong career in education. He studied at Nanjing Higher Normal School, which was renamed Southeastern University about the time he graduated and later became National Central University. The dean at the time was Tao Xingzhi, a professor in the Department of Education, and my father enrolled in this department under Professor Tao's influence. After graduation, he was employed by this school as a teaching assistant and later a lecturer, before becoming a professor at Lantian Normal College in Hunan.

After WWII, my father returned to Nanjing and served as director of inspection in the municipal Bureau of Education and president of the Nanjing Municipal Normal School, and eventually returned to the Department of Education of Central University as a professor. One of his schoolmates at Anhui Second Normal School and Nanjing Higher Normal School, Ke Qingshi, was very poor and was often subsidized by my father. Ke Qingshi participated in underground CCP activities, rose up in the CCP, and became vice mayor of Nanjing after the communist takeover. Because of my father's friendship with Ke Qingshi, and also owing to my father's protection of students who were underground CCP members from arrest by the KMT government when he was Nanjing Municipal Normal School president, my father was well treated by the CCP regime and was arranged to become a delegate to the first People's Congress of the municipality in 1954. Later, he was persuaded by the China Democratic League to join this party. Actually, my father didn't care much about politics and only aspired to better the nation via education, focusing entirely on teaching and operating schools. Since he was considered a pro-CCP democratic figure, he was often invited by the UFWD to attend conferences and participate in tours and studies. I learned from him that the UFWD was in charge of non-CCP intellectuals like himself, but I knew nothing about other functions of the UFWD.

Mr. Zhang took me to all the offices in the building. The last of these was the office of the Political Parties Division, where I would work. I was greeted by three coworkers, who all happened to be women. Mr. Zhang introduced me to a lady in her forties, who was slightly overweight and wore a pair of golden-frame spectacles. This was Ms. Shen, the division director. Again, Mr. Zhang advised me to learn as much as possible from my colleagues, and then left.

Indicating one of the desks, Ms. Shen told me this would be my desk, and that I would officially start work tomorrow. This was the beginning of my career at the UFWD.

Chapter 3: Colleagues with Legendary Experiences

Heroines in the Political Parties Division

The full name of my division is Division of Democratic Political Parties Work. It is an internal organ of the UWFD in charge of monitoring minor political parties and intellectuals. When introducing me to my other two colleagues, Director Shen joked that with the arrival of a male colleague, our division had undergone a structural transformation and, starting today, would no longer be a women's association. As elder sisters we should take care of our little brother, who in turn should learn from his elder sisters and do his modest best for our division. We all laughed, myself feeling embarrassed in front of these older, very experienced colleagues. I indicated that I knew nothing about United Front work and would have to rely on their help and patience in the months ahead.

When I got to know my new colleagues better, I learned that all three had had extraordinary experiences during the Communist Revolution. For example, although Director Shen appeared as gentle as a middle school teacher, she was actually a senior member of the CCP who joined the Revolution during the early phase of WWII. She was born into an elite family in Shanghai, but had already begun to participate in underground CCP activities while in high school. She was a passionate patriot who couldn't endure the Japanese occupation. In 1940, she was dispatched by the underground CCP branch in Shanghai to the New Fourth Army's base area in northern Jiangsu Province. She worked in the political unit of the military and later married her superior officer, the director of the Organization Division. He was an old cadre from Shandong Province who finished middle school (with this level of education, one could be called an intellectual at the time), had good political fortunes and was already a division-level officer when the PLA marched south. He later became the director general of the military region's Political Department with the rank of senior colonel at deputy commander level. As a high-level officer, he lived in a mansion and had a dedicated chauffeur. There were two nannies in his household to take care of the family's five children, two of whom were still preschoolers.

Due to her elite status and her impressive resume dating back to the WWII era, Ms. Shen's demeanor was always one of pride. Her self-esteem was so high that if she sensed even a hint of disrespect from one of her colleagues, she would remain angry for a day or two. In general, one learned to listen to her deferentially without expressing opinions.

Only later did I learn that this proud revolutionary woman harbored many dark secrets. On a few occasions I observed that her eyelids were swollen but didn't dare to ask why, only to learn later from a female coworker that she was angry at her husband. Naive as I was, I couldn't understand how such an elite family could suffer from internal strife. Later I became aware that, as a passionate, idealistic girl, Ms. Shen was pressured by the Party Organization to marry a higher official with whom she had little in common in terms of cultural interests and lifestyle. Not long after, she found out that her husband was already married in his hometown and had a son.

This daughter of the revolution was understandably enraged when she discovered that she had been deceived. It was said that this came out less than a month after she gave birth to her first child, and she furiously demanded a divorce. Finally, the Party Organization intervened, emphasizing that Party members should have faith in the Party and explaining that "It is the Party's need for you to marry a senior official." Actually, after the Communist takeover, it was not uncommon for high officials of the CCP to "replace" their wives, experiencing a change of heart soon after receiving a promotion. This is very similar to the "keeping-a-mistress" phenomenon prevalent among CCP officials more recently, the precursor of which was already a special privilege of high officials during the revolutionary era.

Perhaps as a result of her personal experiences during the revolution, Director Shen always tended to make decisions independently, never blindly complying with her superiors' dictates. I admired this strong quality in her. She didn't like to repeat other people's words, always asked pertinent questions, and never flattered any of her superiors. She often expressed objections to the statements and actions of "leftists" in minor political parties who distorted facts and cast aspersions on others in order to please the CCP. These characteristics of hers which I admired were not welcomed by her superiors and actually undermined her career. As a result, she remained at the division director level for decades without promotion.

Ms. Yang, another prominent female in the Political Parties Division, was very soon promoted to the position of deputy director. She was 5 feet 11 inches tall with the figure of a super model and the temperament of a noble woman. In an era when almost everyone wore Chinese tunic suits in plain indigo, she sometimes wore cheongsam with a red cropped cardigan sweater and a light-colored silk scarf. We often jokingly told her that she could play the role of a revolutionary heroine on the stage and wouldn't need to wear any makeup. At the time, she was already nearly forty but still very beautiful and engaging. Her large eyes always carried a hint of a mysterious smile, and when she looked at you straight in the eye, it was hard not to be enchanted by her.

Over ten years earlier, Ms. Yang was a highly skilled spy of the CCP. As a student at Southwest United University in Kunming near the end of WWII, she dated and cohabited with a fellow student who was a leader of the university's student movement and an underground CCP member. Her boyfriend succumbed to lung disease, and Ms. Yang became a popular "student widow," pursued by many elite and affluent men. The CCP identified her as spy material and recruited her into its military intelligence system. During the Chinese Civil War, she directly reported to the military intelligence unit of the CCP's Second Field Army and was tasked with gathering the KMT's confidential military information. Thanks to her good looks and excellent social skills, she was soon very much at home in high-level KMT circles. She transferred to Central University in Nanjing when it was restored after WWII. She liked to joke that while other people spent four years in college, she had spent eight, and her student status was actually a cover-up of her espionage activities.

Two months before the CCP takeover of Nanjing, Ms. Yang was dispatched to Kunming so that the Party could take advantage of her social connections in Kunming to collect military intelligence there in preparation for urging the governor of Yunnan Province, Lu Han, to defect to the CCP. She lived in the home of a high-level KMT military officer and the liaison between her and the underground CCP was disguised as a cigarette vendor on the street from whom she often bought cigarettes. This liaison, who was also her superior officer, was formerly a cadre of the Eighth Route Army and was dispatched there to carry out espionage activities. He and Ms. Yang were both credited with enabling the CCP's peaceful takeover of Yunnan. They were transferred to Nanjing and were soon married. Her husband was made Director of the Political Department of Nanjing Military College and later attained the rank of colonel at division level. Ms. Yang left the military and was assigned to the UFWD.

One of the tasks of our Political Parties Division was to detect political trends by constantly tracking the political expressions and activities of the targets of United Front work, especially their leaders. With her training and experience in espionage, Ms. Yang excelled at this type of work. She had good connections to many democratic figures and always seemed to be the first to uncover information. Her superiors would reflexively shout, "Send for Yang!" whenever an investigation wasn't showing results. After the Anti-Rightist Campaign, Ms. Yang got into the strange habit of frequently taking a small notebook out of her purse and announcing that she was going to "sort out their sequence." Beside a list of 40 to 50 leaders of minor political parties in her notebook, she would attach labels such as leftist, center-leftist, centrist, center-rightist, and rightist. The same person might be labeled "leftist" at a given time and "center-leftist" at other times. I had difficulty understanding how a person's political status could change every several days and didn't grasp the point of this process of labeling and relabeling. However, she claimed that this method of sorting to analyze targets had always proven accurate and had met with the approval of her superiors.

Ms. Yang's extraordinary accomplishments rank with those of other successful espionage activities carried out by famous female spies in history. For many men, a woman's special charm can be a fatal weakness, hence the expression "The hero becomes a prisoner of love."

Ms. Yang was not universally liked, however. In fact, another United Front officer, a section-level cadre named Ms. Guo, despised her attractive coworker. Although she could never compete with Ms. Yang in terms of external appearance, she was much better at writing. She often teased Ms. Yang that, despite her college education and her degree in economics, her writing was not up to the level of a high school student's. Apparently, Ms. Yang had been too busy collecting intelligence information to spend much time on academics.

I once jokingly suggested to Ms. Guo that Ms. Yang must have made many male friends while carrying out her espionage work. What would she do if a high-level KMT official made sexual advances toward her? Ms. Guo casually answered that it was no problem if it was done for the sake of an important assignment. Coming at a sexually conservative time, such an answer surprised me. I concluded that female spies must have a somewhat liberal attitude toward sex, seeing it as permissible as long as one didn't become emotionally involved.

Ms. Guo was an amazing revolutionary woman in her own right. She grew up in a small rural township and fell in love with a young military officer of the KMT when she was 16 years old. Out of rage when this officer deserted her, she enlisted as a CCP guerrilla in a unit which later became part of the New Fourth Army. Although she had only completed the seventh grade in school, she was highly motivated to improve her education and continued to study while in the military. When I joined the UFWD, she was attending adult education classes in the evening and eventually reached college-level literacy. Her writing was of extremely high quality.

I respected my female coworkers as if they were from an older generation. I was grateful for their help and explanations. Since I had been studying and working at schools for so long, I behaved like a student, could not conceal my feelings and had little experience negotiating and solving problems. With the help of my three elder sisters, I improved greatly in these regards.

Cadre Structure of the UFWD

Cadres of the UFWD of the Nanjing municipal CCP Committee mainly consisted of senior CCP members who carried out underground work before the communist takeover.

The three aforementioned colleagues in the Business Sector Division had all done underground work in Nanjing for many years. Its director, Mr. Zhang, transferred from Chongqing to Nanjing after the victory over Japan and got a job at the Puzhen Engine Plant, where he led an underground labor movement using his employment as a disguise. The Puzhen Engine Plant was a subsidiary of the KMT government's Railroad Ministry and employed over a thousand workers. It had important political influence, and its workers cooperated with the PLA and offered important assistance to the

Yangtze River Crossing Campaign. One of the officers of this division had participated in the underground labor union at the Central Emporium. This department store was one of the largest businesses in Nanjing and highly influential at the time. The leader of its underground union, Mr. Qiu, became director of the Commerce Bureau of the municipal government after the communist takeover, which suggests that the union must have had significant influence. Another officer was formerly a high school teacher and underground CCP member who had led a student movement at school. He had lost contact with the Party for a year and had been a target of review and examination during all the subsequent rectifications and political movements of the CCP. Since he could never explain to the satisfaction of the Party why he had been out of contact for one year, he never received a promotion.

A colleague who transferred to the UFWD after me liked to joke that our organization had a mix of people from the manufacturing, commerce, education, and military sectors and only lacked someone from the agricultural field. He himself had been a peasant before joining the military, so he could represent the agricultural sector and fill the void. In fact, he later became director of the Office of Rightist Transformation Work. The reasoning must have been that a peasant in charge of "rightists" would treat them all as class enemies. The UFWD had learned to make effective use of its personnel resources and cadres were assigned to positions based on their relevant qualifications.

During the early days after the communist takeover, the leaders of the Nanjing municipal UWFD were almost all former underground CCP cadres. The director general had been Shi Yong, a former CCP spy in the KMT government whose elder brother, Sha Wenhan, would later become governor of Zhejiang Province. Sha's wife, Chen Xiuliang, was a legendary underground CCP figure who carried out underground work in Nanjing during WWII and the Civil War and once held the position of Secretary of the Nanjing municipal CCP Committee. Unfortunately, these two senior intellectual cadres were both labeled as rightists during the Anti-Rightist Campaign. Sha died before the Cultural Revolution, while Chen survived and was given a deputy minister-level position as an advisor to the Shanghai Academy of Social Sciences. As for Shi, he later transferred to the national PCC and served as its deputy secretary general until his retirement.

The director general at the time of my entry into the UFWD, Mr. Wang, was also a former underground cadre who came to Nanjing during WWII together with Chen Xiuliang.

One of the deputy directors general, Mr. Ma, was an even more legendary figure. He was formerly a trolley conductor and an underground CCP member at the beginning of WWII and carried out underground activities while in the Shanghai Trolley Labor Union. In 1939, the underground CCP organization in Nanjing was exposed and almost its members arrested. The municipal Party secretary was executed by firing squad. In order to reestablish the underground CCP organization in Nanjing, the Central Committee decided to transfer a few cadres from Shanghai to Nanjing to restart activities. Mr. Ma was among them and entered Nanjing at this time. The Party funded a grain store at Xiaguan Harbor with Mr. Ma as its nominal owner, using it as a front to facilitate communications and personnel transportations between the New Fourth Army north of the Yangtze River and the underground CCP organization south of the river. During WWII, CCP leader Liu Shaoqi and three leading officials of the underground CCP committee in Shanghai all travelled via Ma's arrangements between the north and the south. To ensure the communication hub's security, Ma made many friends among the military, police, and intelligence officials of the pro-Japanese Wang regime and later the KMT regime. The famous "Boss Ma" of Xiaguan Harbor had diverse connections among mafia members as well. Since he was very well disguised, before Nanjing's fall to the communists, the Party decided to dispatch him to Taiwan as a spy to prepare for the eventual invasion of Taiwan. Ma and his family moved to Keelung, Taiwan, in 1948 and temporarily lived in the home of a high intelligence official of the KMT. In 1950, *Xinhua Daily* in Nanjing reported the news that the former secretary of the underground Central Emporium labor union, Mr. Qiu, was named director of the municipal Commerce Bureau. This attracted the attention of the KMT's intelligence agency in Taiwan, because Qiu was formerly an employee in Mr. Ma's store. Taiwan's intelligence agency began to investigate Ma, who learned about this shortly after and notified his superiors. The underground CCP organization in Taiwan decided to immediately move Ma back to mainland China in order to protect him. Ma and his family soon fled to Hong Kong and from there back to Nanjing, where he was named deputy director general of the municipal UFWD with Administrative Rank 13 compensation. (Note that those with a rank of 13 or higher were considered high-level cadres).

Ma's legendary experiences had negative consequences during the Cultural Revolution. He was constantly under investigation by the Rebels and questioned as to why he lived in the home of a KMT intelligence official, why he made contact with KMT military and police officials during his underground work, and whether he had leaked Party secrets. At one point, when Ma could no longer tolerate the denunciation, he asked the rebels why the underground CCP heroine Aqing in the revolutionary opera *Shajiabang* saved the militia leader Hu Chuanqui, a non-CCP figure who later cooperated with the Japanese. The Rebels accused Ma of badmouthing a revolutionary opera and elevated their denunciation of him to major-assembly level. As a result, Ma suffered greatly.

Ma began as a laborer and only completed the seventh grade in school. After he became deputy director general, he still possessed only a rudimentary level of theoretical knowledge and had to rely on speechwriters to prepare his speeches. Once he had to attend two meetings on the same day, one in the morning and the other in the afternoon. In the morning, he got his manuscripts switched and began reading the text that had been prepared for the afternoon. He didn't realize the mistake until several paragraphs into it and hastily switched to the correct script.

When Ma was in charge of the underground communication and transportation hub, because of the importance of his work, the Party ensured that he lived the luxurious life of a successful business owner, playing mahjong all day long and enjoying meat and liquor every day. However, after his underground work was terminated, with his wife being a homemaker and all five of his children still in school, he became economically distressed despite his Rank 13 compensation, and the Party Organization had to grant him a special subsidy. His standard of living was especially low during the three years of famine, when he often had to go without meat or liquor. He often complained and hence was always denounced in political movements for his fondness of his bourgeois past. He became a laughingstock in the Party institutions for "contrasting his happiness in the old era with his sufferings in the new one," at a time when the comparison should have been the other way around.

On the other hand, some senior cadres from old revolutionary base areas of the CCP and the military were also transferred into the UFWD to serve in leadership positions after the establishment of the communist regime. The administrative deputy director general of the Nanjing municipal CCP Committee UFWD, Ms. Wang, had once been such a senior cadre from the revolutionary base in northern Jiangsu Province, where she had been an elementary school teacher before joining the New Fourth Army during WWII to conduct guerrilla warfare. She was very outspoken and candid, didn't bother as much about formalities as other senior cadres, and had a reputation for being concerned about employees' difficulties.

After learning of my colleagues' unusual past experiences, I came to respect them for their ardor in fulfilling their duties and appreciated the insight they were able to give me into the operations of the UFWD.

Chapter 4: What Does the UFWD Do?

For most Chinese people, the UFWD exists behind a veil of mystery. As an inner organ of the CCP, it coordinates the activities of several external organizations, including the PCC, the People's Congress, minor political parties, and various social organizations. It is an example of "the insider knowing the ropes while the outsider is just along for the ride." I myself knew very little about the UFWD before joining.

When Mao Zedong summarized the CCP's historical experiences under his leadership, he proudly said:

> *The United Front, armed struggle, and Party building are the three secret weapons that the Chinese Communist Party deploys to defeat enemies in the Chinese revolution.   Correctly understanding these three programs and their inter-relationships is essential to correctly leading the Chinese revolution.*

In plain words, Mao was telling his political opponents that in all China only he was in control of these three essential weapons and hence the revolution he was leading would eventually succeed. After 22 years of intense fighting, he finally drove the KMT regime out of mainland China.

Mao's description of the United Front as a "secret weapon" of the CCP is central to understanding United Front work. This can be demonstrated in three ways:

First, throughout history the ability to form alliances has been a political skill that has characterized every successful leader. In China, Emperor Liu Bang of the Han Dynasty (with his strategist Zhang Liang), Emperor Liu Bei of the Three Kingdoms Period (with his strategist Zhuge Liang), and Emperor Zhu Yuanzhang of the Ming Dynasty (with his strategist Liu Bowen) were all skilled at forming alliances with the intention of defeating opponents before they succeeded in establishing their reign.

In terms of modern revolutionary movements, Lenin was the first proponent in the theory and practice of a "united front" and played an unparalleled role in the dissemination of the united front strategy and its application. According to Leninist theory, the united front is a political alliance that the proletariat forms with different political factions, parties, and other forces that can be consociated on the basis of common interests under certain historical conditions in order to fulfill its strategic political responsibilities and achieve its goals. In simple terms, the united front is a form of political alliance.

Why did Mao first mention the United Front as one of the CCP's "three secret weapons"? Clearly, he understood the importance of the United Front as the No. 1 "secret weapon," which is consistent with his other mantra, "Politics is in command and is the soul."

In the several thousand years of Chinese history, we find that those who ascended to the throne via peasant revolutions were successful not only militarily but, more importantly, in terms of making political alliances. This is what the ancient historians meant when they described these powerful leaders as having "civil expertise and military strategies." If successful only in the military arena, such strongmen inevitably ended up as failures.

How was Lenin able to seize power in Russia, where the population consisted mainly of peasants, and establish the first communist regime in the world? It could be considered a success of Lenin's united front strategy. He grasped a favorable historical opportunity and took advantage of the Russian Provisional Government's mistaken World War I policy and the anti-war sentiment among the people and the armed forces to carry out a military coup d'état. After the initial success of the October Revolution, he took advantage of the continuing military conflict and negotiated peace with Germany so that he could stabilize his regime, eliminate hostile domestic military forces, and establish a totalitarian state under a communist dictatorship. Lenin said the following about the united front in *"Left Wing" Communism: An Infantile Disorder*:

> *To overcome so potent an enemy is possible only through the greatest effort and by dint of the obligatory, thorough, careful, attentive and skillful utilization of every breach, however small, between the enemies; of every clash of interests between the bourgeoisie of all countries, between various groups and species of bourgeoisie within individual countries;*

of every possibility, however small, of gaining an ally, even though he be temporary, shaky, unstable, unreliable and conditional.... All this applies equally to the period before and after the conquest of political power by the proletariat.

In other words, Lenin identified two types of allies: one made up of all sympathetic forces that can be united, and one formed by exploiting all conflicts within enemy camps. In ***"Left-Wing" Communism***, Lenin also emphasized that *"It is necessary to coordinate the strictest devotion to the ideas of Communism with the ability to accept all necessary practical compromises, maneuvering, temporizing, zig-zags, retreats and the like."* Lenin's words above demonstrate his remarkable understanding of the united front strategy. If the united front is a political trick, then the goal is fixed while the strategies and tactics can be very flexible and sometimes even devious. In other words, if you want to catch the fox, you have to be more cunning than the fox.

Judging from the history of the CCP's development, its United Front was cultivated under Soviet instructions, and the best student of Lenin's united front strategy was not one of those intellectuals who had studied abroad and visited the Soviet Union but Mao Zedong, a country bumpkin and petty intellectual. Mao mastered the united front strategy at all times and in all places and was especially adept at learning from failures. He knew ***Romance of the Three Kingdoms*** by heart, a book of stories depicting cunning strategies, and was not dogmatic but able to adapt to various local conditions.

It is an historical fact that intellectuals such as Chen Duxiu, Zhang Guotao, and Zhou Fohai, who attended the CCP's First National Congress, distained united front activities and wrote the following in the Party Charter:

The revolutionary armed forces must join force with the proletariat to overthrow the bourgeoisie's regime, ... accept the dictatorship of the proletariat until class struggles are ended, ... eliminate the bourgeoisie's institution of private ownership, ... join forces with the Communist International, ... and completely sever all connections to the bourgeoisie-

leaning intellectual class and other similar political parties and factions.

From this historical document, we can conclude that the CCP leadership at that time was extremely naïve concerning the issue of a united front, a reflection of the leftist revolutionary fervor of many intellectuals at that time. The Party Charter captivated Russian communist leaders, including Lenin himself. After the Conference of Far East Countries' Communist Parties and National Revolutionary Groups in February 1922, Lenin met with the CCP delegation and requested that CCP leaders cooperate with the KMT and advance the revolutionary war together to unite China. As a revolutionary intellectual, Chen Duxiu still had difficulty accepting the policy of CCP members joining the KMT. Later, the Communist International authorized Maring and his aid and interpreter, Zhang Tailei, to directly enjoin the CCP's implementation of the united front strategy. The CCP's Second National Congress in July 1922 passed a resolution to form an allied democratic front, and its Third National Congress in June 1923 decided that CCP members should join the KMT on an individual basis. That same year the executive committee of the Communist International passed the Resolution on the Relationship between the CCP and the KMT. As for the KMT, Sun Yat-sen and Soviet convoy Adolph Joffe issued the Joint Manifesto of Sun and Joffe, asserting that the Soviet institutions were not suitable for China and that Russia did not seek the independence of Outer Mongolia. At this point, the KMT and the CCP began to cooperate. This policy of the KMT was referred to as "Allying with Russia and Tolerating the CCP," but the CCP later distorted this to "The Three Major Policies of Allying with Russia, Allying with the CCP, and Supporting Peasants and Workers."

After the success of the Northern Expedition and the KMT's crackdown on the CCP, because of intra-party factional conflicts, Chen Duxiu and his associates were accused of being rightists and expelled from CCP leadership. Leftist intellectuals wielded power in the CCP and carried out urban uprisings, all of which failed after being harshly suppressed. CCP organizations in KMT-ruled areas were almost completely destroyed, and CCP leadership was forced to retreat to its rural base area in Jiangxi Province, where it failed again because of internal conflicts and the dogmatic military command of the Communist International's delegate. This led to the so-called "Long March" to the northwest, which was actually an escape. Not until 1935 did the CCP secure its base area in Northwest China when its leadership, headed by Mao Zedong, adopted the strategy of "establishing the widest Anti-Japanese National United Front" under the Communist International's strategic directive to create an international anti-fascist united front. At a 1935 CCP Central Committee conference in Wayaobu, Shanxi Province, Mao Zedong gave an incisive talk on the United Front. Summarizing the experiences and lessons of the CCP's failure in the civil war during the previous decade, he said, "*We must exploit all the conflicts, breaches, and confrontations among the enemy camps and use them to fight our main enemy.*" This indicated Mao had truly grasped the significance of Leninism on the issue of a united front and had become the main proponent of the CCP's united front strategy.

The second most enthusiastic supporter of the CCP's United Front was none other than Zhou Enlai, the organizer and implementer of the CCP's United Front strategy and a political strategist who overcame numerous early failures. The highlight of his political career was not his premiership of the CCP regime but his leading role in the negotiations between the CCP and the KMT before and after China's victory over Japan. His performance was extremely skillful and unparalleled by any other politician in modern Chinese history. At the CCP's Seventh National Congress, which took place from April to June 1945, Zhou gave a talk on the United Front in which he divided the CCP's struggle against the KMT over the past 15 years into five stages in order to analyze the key methods of defeating the KMT. He summarized the objectives of the United Front as "*seeking common ground while accepting differences; united while independent; allied while fighting; insisting on self-rule while accepting external aid.*" This talk was clear proof that the CCP's United Front strategy had reached maturity. As a consequence, the tragic fate of the KMT was sealed, and the CCP completely outsmarted the KMT during the subsequent years and achieved a decisive victory in the Chinese Civil War.

The revolution's two strategies, United Front and armed struggle, are complementary to each other, one functioning as the right hand and the other the left. Mao famously said that "political power grows out of the barrel of a gun" and Red China was created by military means. But Mao should never be dismissed as simply a military strongman who came to power and ruled through sheer force. Chinese emperors who overthrew dynasties and assumed the throne via armed rebellion understood that a peaceful rebellion had no chance of success. However, although military force is a crucial factor in any rebellion, if one only knows how to fight and not how to govern strategically, failure is inevitable. Such heroic figures as Xiang Yu, Li Zicheng, and Hong Xiuquan failed to implement a united front strategy and all ended up as tragic failures.

The role of the United Front in the CCP's history of armed struggle had two aspects. The first was to divide and incite the defection of enemies, taking advantage of their factional and personnel conflicts, central and local differences, and mafia-like internal cliques.

During the early years of the so-called "Agrarian Revolutionary War" (1927-1937), the CCP was not adept at creating rifts among enemies or collecting intelligence information and focused instead on waging head-to-head battles against the KMT. The CCP paid a heavy price for its initial failure to understand the importance of espionage work. Near the end of the "Agrarian Revolutionary War," the CCP Central Committee required that all levels of Party Organizations and all its armed forces establish "backstage work" committees or units, which were essentially in charge of military intelligence and inciting the defection of enemy forces. The Intelligence Department of the CCP central committee was established in 1941, and the Urban Work Department was established shortly before the victory over Japan and later renamed the United Front Work Department. As mentioned in the previous chapter, many UFWD employees during the early years after the establishment of the CCP regime in 1949 were former spies, due to the historical ties between the United Front and the military intelligence work of the CCP.

During the Chinese Civil War that followed WWII, the United Front work that the CCP carried out to gather intelligence from KMT military commanders played a very important role in the CCP's victory. Large-scale defections of KMT armed forces took place on ten occasions, which enabled the CCP to completely dominate the war. For example, the defections of Wu Huawen, Zeng Zesheng, and Fu Zuoyi quickly shifted the balance of power in the war zones of northeastern and northern China, and those of Cheng Qian, Chen

Mingren, Lu Han, Dong Qiwu, and Tao Zhiyue were crucial to the CCP's unification of mainland China.

The CCP's intelligence work was also very successful, to the extent that classified military information of the KMT government's Defense Department quickly found its way to the desks of CCP leaders, while the KMT had no idea about CCP force deployment.

The other aspect of United Front work in the CCP's armed struggles was that of propaganda, consociation, and economic incentives to the masses in battle zones, tactics which the CCP learned through experience. Earlier, when it established bases as so-called "soviet areas," its ultra-left policy of turning petty bourgeoisie into proletariat in order to force them to join the revolution was greatly distained by the masses, which isolated CCP forces and created conditions beneficial to KMT forces. As Zhou Enlai put it when summarizing the relationship between the United Front and armed struggles during the civil war, "*To establish a solidified United Front of the new democracy is to correctly recognize the contradictions during the process of historical development and to constantly identify and analyze enemies....To win over the majority, we need well-organized allies and specific solutions based on specific situations.*" As he went on to explain: "*Right-leaning opportunism is to give away allies and left-leaning opportunism is to push away allies; both cause damage to the revolution.*" Zhou Enlai also confessed that he had made mistakes in negotiations with Deng Yanda's "Third Party," saying that Deng Yanda reached out to the CCP to negotiate an anti-Chiang Kai-shek alliance, but Zhou didn't respond at all and lost this potential ally. He also committed this same error of "shutting the door" when the 19th Route Army attempted to establish a democratic government in Fujian Province.

What exactly is the relationship between the United Front and Party building? Mao Zedong didn't elaborate on this, and Zhou Enlai intentionally avoided the topic. The reason for this is that most people, including many CCP members, view the United Front as between the Party and external political forces, and it is taboo to discuss whether United Front strategy is applicable to intra-Party political struggles. Mao himself suggested that whoever was able to understand the relationships between the United Front, armed struggle, and Party building was destined to lead the Chinese revolution. This implies that the relationship between the United Front and Party building was a close one.

When analyzing Mao's words, it is necessary to understand what he meant by "Party building." There is good reason to believe that, for Mao, Party building was not limited to a tight and disciplined Party organization but, more importantly, an authoritative, unified, and stable leadership. Such authoritative leadership resulted from numerous intra-party conflicts that weeded out various factions and political oppositions. This leadership was not only the architect of the Party's united front strategy but also the successful implementer of this strategy in intra-party conflicts.

Ever since the founding of the CCP, intra-party factional conflicts existed. Conflicts between intellectual elites and Party leaders who came from the working and peasant classes on the adaptation of Marxism-Leninism to Chinese conditions erupted from the beginning, and these conflicts had a lot to do with the United Front strategy that emerged. What's more, the intervention of the Communist International created a rift between foreign-educated individuals and local factions. Mao adopted a flexible strategy which adopted the innovative approach of creating revolutionary bases in rural areas and cultivating an armed force under his control, while watching the conflict among Party leadership as a bystander. Eventually, the CCP leadership could no longer survive in Shanghai because of internal conflicts and a crackdown conducted by the KMT government. The CCP relocated to the rural areas controlled by Mao, who deployed the tactic of "divide and conquer" on his former bosses. Mao focused his resources on attacking those foreign-educated elites who, carrying the banner of the Communist International, controlled Party affairs behind the scenes. His strategy was to lure them into a false sense of security before strangling them and to retreat before launching an offensive. During the struggle to expose and criticize the "leftist dogmatism" of Bo Gu and Otto Braun, he won over Zhou Enlai and also used Zhang Wentian to concentrate Party powers in his own hands.

Mao successfully applied the United Front strategy to intra-party politics after he ascended to the top position in the CCP. He conducted the Yan'an Rectification Movement and developed a method of punishing political opponents using mass movements. He first called for criticism and self-criticism of opponents and then led public opinion in the direction of mass criticism, completely isolating and defeating his opponents.

Once mainland China was completely under communist rule, Mao continued to use the united front strategy and rectification movements to punish political opponents and dissidents outside the Party first and then defeat opponents within the Party one by one. His habitual tactics were to retreat before advancing, "entice a snake out of its hole," mobilize the masses, and encircle and destroy the enemy. These same political stratagems have been passed on to his successors.

In summary, the relationship between Mao Zedong's so-called three secret weapons is illustrated in the following analogy: The United Front and armed struggle are like your two hands: They must cooperate in order to defeat the enemy. The hand that is the United Front can detect and identify the opponent's vulnerabilities, so that the other hand can launch a lethal blow. Party building, on the other hand, is perhaps even more crucial and can be likened to the brain. If the brain lacks a unified will, it will be unable to issue consistent commands, direct the hands' movements, or distinguish between friends and foes.

Chapter 5: Minor Political Parties "Listen, Follow, and Stride"

One of the important tasks of the CCP's UFWD was to manage minor political parties. Therefore, all provincial and municipal-level UFWDs had a "Division of Democratic Political Parties Work," commonly known as the "Political Parties Division." After I belonged to the UWFD, I spent over six years in this division, and hence became very familiar with the operations of minor political parties.

First, I'd like to provide a basic introduction to the minor political parties presently active in China. There are eight so-called "democratic political parties" in China: The China Democratic League, the China Association for Promoting Democracy, the Chinese Peasants' and Workers' Democratic Party, the Revolutionary Committee of the Chinese Kuomintang, the Jiusan Society, the China Zhi Gong Party, the China National Democratic Construction Association, and the Taiwan Democratic Self-Government League. Many of these parties were formed in KMT-ruled areas toward the end of WWII. Their historical background is as follows:

1. The China Democratic League (CDL) was formed secretly as the League of Chinese Democratic Political Organizations in Chongqing on March 19, 1941, and adopted its current name in 1944. Its precursor, Solidarity for Unified State Building, was founded by members of the National Political Participation Conference in November 1939. Founding constituent organizations of the CDL included the Chinese Youth Party and the National Socialist Party (which was unrelated to the German Nazi party and later renamed the Chinese Democratic Socialist Party). The two aforementioned parties later opposed leftists, supported the KMT government, and participated in the National Constituent Assembly in 1946, which led to their being excluded from the CDL, labeled as "reactionary organizations" by the CCP, and exiled to Taiwan together with the KMT government. Other founding members of the CDL included the Chinese Action Committee for National Liberation (which later became the Chinese Peasants' and Workers' Democratic Party and split from the CDL in 1947), the National Vocational Education Society, the National Rural Reconstruction Association, and the

44

National Salvation Association. Huang Yanpei was chosen to be the first chairman of the CDL's central committee; after Huang's resignation, he was replaced by Zhang Lan. They exhorted their membership to "Oppose Dictatorship and Demand Democracy; Oppose Civil War and Demand Peace." During negotiations between the CCP and the KMT, the CDL steered public opinion in favor of the CCP. In addition, they were influential in supporting the anti-Chiang and anti-KMT movements. The CDL was outlawed by the KMT government in 1947. The following year, its Third Plenary Session of the First Central Committee was held in Hong Kong, where the CDL publicly declared its cooperation with the CCP and called for the overthrow of the KMT regime. After the communist regime was established in mainland China in 1949, CDL chairman Zhang Lan became one of the vice chairs of the Central People's Government under Chairman Mao. The CDL's main constituents are intellectuals.

2. The Revolutionary Committee of the Chinese Kuomintang (RCCK) began as two anti-Chiang factions of the KMT, the Federation of Comrades of the Three-People's Principles, formed in Chongqing in 1945, and the Democracy Promotion Council of the KMT, formed in Guangzhou in 1946. They joined forces to hold the First Joint Conference of Democratic Factions of the KMT in Hong Kong in November 1947, and the conference declared the founding of the Revolutionary Committee of the KMT on January 1, 1948 with Song Qingling as its chairperson of honor, Li Jishen as its chairperson, and He Xiangning and Feng Yuxiang among its leadership. When the CCP regime was established in 1949, Song Qingling and Li Jishen became vice chairs of the Central People's Government. The RCCK's principal constituents are former political and military officials of the KMT regime who remained on the mainland, and their decedents.

3. The Chinese Peasants' and Workers' Democratic Party (CPWDP) is the oldest among the eight minor political parties. Its precursor was the Provisional Action Committee of the KMT founded by Deng Yanda in 1930, who advocated a "third way" of Chinese politics and was executed by Chiang Kai-shek in 1931. Its key leaders included Huang Qixiang, Zhang Bojun, Peng Zemin, and Ji Fang. It was formerly a part of the CDL, and was reestablished under its current name in Shanghai in 1947. Its constituents are mainly medical and engineering professionals.

4. The China Association for Promoting Democracy (CAPD) is a party consisting of mainly mid- to high-level intellectuals in the education, culture, and publishing sectors. The majority of its founding members—including Ma Xulun, Wang Shaoao, Zhou Jianren, Xu Guangping, Lin Handa, Xu Boxin, Zhao Puchu, Lei Jieqiong, Zhen Zhenduo, and Ke Ling—were intellectuals in the fields of education and culture who remained in Shanghai during WWII and participated in anti-Japanese activities with assistance from underground CCP members. After the victory over Japan, they participated in movements against the KMT government and decided to form a political organization with the aim of "carrying forward the spirit of democracy and promoting the realization of democratic politics in China," calling themselves the China Association for Promoting Democracy. In 1946, sixty-eight organizations in Shanghai were brought together by the underground CCP municipal committee to form the Federation of Shanghai People's Organizations. A demonstration of over 100,000 people was held on June 23 of that year and a delegation which included CAPD leaders Ma Xulun and Lei Jieqiong was sent to Nanjing to petition the KMT government. The delegates were badly beaten at Xiaguan Railroad Station in Nanjing, in what came to be known as the Xiaguan Incident. After the establishment of the CCP regime, Xu Guangping, Zhou Jianren, and Lei Jieqiong were assigned to leadership positions in the People's Congress and the PCC.

5. The Jiusan Society's precursor was the Democracy and Science Forum, organized by a few intellectuals in the science and technology sectors in Chongqing toward the end of WWII. It assumed its current name to commemorate the date of Chinese victory in WWII (September 3, 1945) and was officially formed on May 4, 1946. The majority of its constituents are intellectuals in higher education and research institutions.

6. The China Zhi Gong Party was formed in October 1925 in San Francisco by the American Zhi Gong Tang. Its first party congress elected Chen Jiongming and Tang Jiyao as premier and vice premier of the party. It helped to protect the rights of the Chinese diaspora overseas and supported China's anti-Japanese war efforts during WWII. Its third party congress was held in Hong Kong in May 1947 and declared support for the CCP. Its main constituents include

overseas Chinese who returned to China and relatives of overseas Chinese.

7. The China National Democratic Construction Association (CNDCA) was formed in Chongqing on December 16, 1945 by Huang Yanpei, Hu Juewen, Zhang Naiqi, Shi Fuliang, Sun Qimeng, among others, with entrepreneurs and intellectuals as its main constituents. In 1953, the CCP arranged for the formation of the All-China Federation of Industry and Commerce (ACFIC) to enhance its control over the private economy and prepare for the nationalization of the latter. Business people who were not members of the CNDCA were absorbed into the ACFIC. In fact, these two organizations share much of the same leadership. They are well known as the "Two Organizations" in the business sector. Also, the United Front work of the CNDCA is overseen by the Business Sector Division of the UFWD, rather than by the Political Parties Division.

8. The Taiwan Democratic Self-Government League was formed in Hong Kong on November 12, 1947, by Taiwan Communist Party members for the purpose of subverting the KMT's rule in Taiwan and inciting defections. Its early leaders, including Xie Xuehong, were all underground CCP members in Taiwan. Because of the KMT government's crackdown, it couldn't survive in Taiwan and was forced to retreat to mainland China.

It was three years after the end of the Anti-Rightist Campaign (which lasted from 1957 to 1958) when I entered the UFWD. I soon found out that minor political parties were all in very low spirits. Most of their members kept a distance from the CCP because they saw that many outspoken people were labeled as rightists and suffered greatly. Once they had discovered how formidable the CCP was, they rejoiced at having survived the campaign without being labeled as rightists. After all, who would believe in Mao's assurances that the CCP and minor parties would "coexist for the long term and monitor each other"? Those former underground members of the minor parties who joined before the communist takeover were by and large taken in by Mao Zedong, who, in order to defeat the KMT, spoke a lot of high-flown words about democracy, liberty, and rights and strongly urged intellectuals to demonstrate in the streets to demand democracy and denounce the KMT as bureaucratic and corrupt. I still remember the banners and slogans of student demonstrations in the streets on May 20, 1947, and the huge gathering of students with torches on the campus of Central University that night. It was extremely similar to the street demonstrations and the protests in Tian'anmen Square forty-two years later, the only difference being that the police and security forces of the KMT government didn't dare to open fire on students and only used sticks and water cannons.

After the CCP seized power in mainland China, Mao clearly realized that the nature of the struggle had changed, and that former allies had become obstacles to his dictatorship. To quote Field Marshal Chen Yi when he denounced Peng Dehuai at the Lushan Conference: *"A former meritorious serviceman is a current chief culprit."* When Mao felt the time had come to crack down on minor political parties, he took the opportunity of a rectification campaign of the CCP to call for critical expression. Actually, the purpose was to entice people to voice dissent so that the CCP could then identify and crack down on dissenters. Not until many leaders of minor political parties had been denounced as rightists did they realize that they had been duped by the CCP. One of the arch-rightists, Chu Anping of the CDL, pointed out before the communist takeover that *"Freedom under the KMT's rule is a matter of how much; if the CCP comes into power, freedom will become a matter of existing or not."* Unfortunately, Chu himself still had some delusions about the CCP and ended up as an arch-rightist who was persecuted severely in the Cultural Revolution and disappeared.

During the Anti-Rightist Campaign, about a quarter of the members of minor political parties were labeled as rightists or internally identified as center-rightists without official labeling. According to official documents, over 550,000 people in China were labeled as rightists. Adding to this the many college students, senior high school students, and grammar school teachers who were expelled or sent to labor camps as reactionary students or evildoers and not counted in official statistics, probably over a million people were persecuted in this campaign.

Among the minor political parties, the CDL was the largest and counted many prominent intellectuals among its members, and it was correspondingly most impacted. A "rightist ring" of eight famous professors—including Fei Xiaotong, Pan Guangdan and Luo Longj—were among its leadership, and famous rightist students such as Lin Xiling among its rank and file. Few in the CDL could enjoy a sense of security.

After I was assigned to the UFWD, my first task was to study the trends of minor political party leaders, referred to internally as "trends in class struggle." One method was to collect information from dual-partisans, i.e., undercover CCP members among cadres of minor political parties. They worked in these parties' institutions as full-time employees, and their main task was to promptly report the actions and words of minor party leaders to the UFWD. Their reports were then summarized by the Political Parties Division of the UFWD and written up as documents, which were submitted to the secretary and standing members of the local CCP committee for review. Another method was to solicit reports from leftist members of minor political parties who wanted to join the CCP.

After surviving the Anti-Rightist Campaign, many leaders of minor political parties lived in a constant state of panic. They would keep a distance from leftists among their circles and would always have something good to say about the CCP. In meetings and group studies, they frequently reiterated that they should not neglect self-criticism and should work to improve on their ideologies. For example, a provincial leader of the CDL, Mr. Chen, was a senior democratic figure who joined the underground CDL when he was a student at Southwest Unified University during WWII. He had previously looked down upon CCP cadres who came from rural base areas without much education. During the "enticing the snake" period right before the Anti-Rightist Campaign, he intended to show off his competence and gave a number of talks which became his undoing, resulting in his being labeled a rightist. Since he had some political influence among the minor parties, he was allowed to stay in the CDL as a committee member and receive on-site transformation on his job in the CDL's office as a negative example—as in the cases of Zhang Bojun and Zhang Naiqi in Beijing. After experiencing the CCP's ferocity, he became a humble man who criticized himself at every meeting for "not listening to Chairman Mao's instructions, not following the CCP closely, and not striding resolutely on the path of socialism." This became a mantra of minor political party members later, that they must "listen, follow, and stride." This former professor not only behaved humbly when in the presence of provincial and municipal CCP leaders, but was even highly respectful to junior cadres in the UFWD like myself. When attending symposiums organized by the People's Congress or the PCC or the so-called "biweekly symposiums" organized by provincial and municipal UFWDs, during break times he would bow to UFWD cadres, including junior ones. His behavior often reminded me of the behavior of prisoners in labor camps toward their jailers. I couldn't help but feel sorry for a university professor who had fallen so low. This individual finally got redress following the Cultural Revolution and became a vice chairperson of the provincial PCC. Most minor political party members who were labeled as rightists were not as fortunate. Some were sent to labor camps, where they committed suicide. A female colleague of my father's, an excellent teacher, was labeled an arch-rightist because she criticized the school's CCP branch secretary for being a layman in the field of education. She committed suicide in a labor camp when she was still in her thirties.

As for the leftists in minor political parties, many of them persecuted rightists in order to win political favors. Some frequently submitted secret reports to the UFWD to show their progressiveness, and the UFWD was happy to use these people to monitor the leaders of their parties. At that time, the provincial and municipal presidents of the CAPD committees were both old spinsters, the provincial one being a famous figure who studied in the US and formerly served as president of a university. In order to ease the workload of these two figures, the UFWD arranged for two female cadres of the CAPD who were also unmarried to serve as full-time liaisons. Every time I ran into them while walking or riding a bike to and from work, they would stop me and complain about their targets' trivial lives in order to show that they were close to the CCP and strove to be progressive.

Some members of minor political parties didn't say anything critical of the CCP but were still labeled rightists. Many victims of political movements were simply too naïve and were framed by so-called leftists.

Once I read a summary report of anti-rightist struggles in high schools in Nanjing written by the municipal CCP committee's rectification and anti-rightist leadership team, which appeared in the internal periodical of the central UFWD, *United Front Work*. This report contained statistics on political labeling of high-school teachers in Nanjing who were not CCP members: 7% were labeled as rightists, 27.8% center-rightists, 13% leftists, and the remainder centrists. The practice of assigning non-CCP individuals to one of four categories—rightists, center-rightists, centrists, and leftists—was based on the six criteria to distinguish "flowers" and "poisonous grasses" that Mao Zedong proposed in his essay *How Should Internal Conflicts among the People Be Dealt With?* But these criteria were based mainly on personal preferences of CCP committee secretaries at lower levels. For example, Mr. Zhang of the CPWDP repeatedly denounced his own father, an arch-rightist, during the Anti-Rightist Campaign for the sake of self-protection, but was still labeled as a center-rightist instead of a leftist. Another cadre of the CPWDP, Mr. Guan, was labeled as a leftist because he knew how to flatter UFWD leaders.

My father, who was a university professor and normal school president before the communist takeover and later became a high school teacher, was classified as a center-rightist in the report. I was quite surprised because my father was apolitical (except that he served as a delegate to the municipal People's Congress and was persuaded to join the CDL, serving as the branch chairperson in his school). He never discussed political issues, and I wondered how he could be labeled a center-rightist. Later, I asked my father in a candid conversation what he did during the Anti-Rightist Campaign. He told me that once, when a rectification meeting was held at his school, the school CCP committee secretary who was supposed to chair the meeting suddenly suggested that my father, as a person of virtue and prestige, should chair the meeting, and my father accepted. It was at this meeting that the aforementioned female teacher criticized CCP cadres, resulting in her later being labeled an arch-rightist. In a meeting to denounce this teacher, another teacher who had also said unflattering things about the CCP in the previous meeting attempted to shirk responsibility by framing her colleague, claiming that she had instigated him to talk and that my father also knew this in advance. The female teacher firmly denied this accusation, and my father was greatly surprised and disgusted by these completely false charges. He stated publically that people should seek truth based on the facts. Probably because of this, the CCP committee labeled my father as a center-rightist, whereas the teacher who had falsely accused my father was labeled as a leftist and soon replaced my father as CDL branch chairperson. My father was disheartened by such infighting and deception and once shook his head and observed that "In today's world, mean people are intoxicated by success."

Soon, my father also learned that his distant relative and elementary school classmate, Cheng Shifan, who was previously one of the vice chairpersons of the Anhui provincial PCC, committed suicide after being labeled as a rightist and sent back to his hometown to be transformed through hard labor. Cheng Shifan was in the first graduating class of the Civil Engineering Department of Peiyang University and once served as the chief engineer of the Huainan Coal Mine. As a prominent engineer in China, he led the construction of the Su-Wan Railway from Nanjing to Jixi, Anhui Province and some other railroads inside Anhui, and also helped to supply the New Fourth Army with large amounts of ammunition and medicine during WWII. His son was a senior underground CCP member and served as director general of a department in the provincial government after the communist takeover. Witnessing how such a meritorious serviceman for the CCP was persecuted to death, my father became pessimistic about the future of the nation. His depression deepened during the Cultural Revolution, resulting in his eventually succumbing to a fatal illness.

After the Anti-Rightist Campaign, the UFWD considered the indirect control of minor political parties via leftists insufficient, and increasingly dispatched dual-partisan CCP cadres to lead these parties directly in order to strengthen political control. CCP members who were dispatched to minor political parties included Chu Tunan and Hu Yuzhi to the CDL central committee, Wu Zhen to the position of provincial president of the Jiusan Society, and Ren Chonggao to the provincial presidency of the RCCK.

These CCP members behaved like delegates of the CCP and considered all statements from UFWD cadres as directives from the CCP. All activities of minor political parties had to be approved by the UFWD. Where, in such a policy, was the so-called "monitoring each other"? It was not surprising that a prominent figure of a minor political party said to others privately: "'Coexist for the long term' is true; who dares to 'monitor each other'?" These words were soon reported to the UFWD as a negative interpretation of the CCP's policy on minor political parties.

Since the Anti-Rightist Campaign had just ended three years before I started working at the UFWD, some cadres were still used to the practice of labeling democratic figures on a scale from leftist to rightist. As mentioned in Chapter 3, Ms. Yang of the Political Parties

Division habitually asked me and other members of minor political parties to work with her on the sorting of democratic figures listed in her notebook. She would label one figure as a "center-rightist" and another as a "center-leftist," etc., but never came up with a "rightist" label on her own because only the municipal CCP committee had the power to label anyone as such. She justified this practice as an important means of grasping the dynamics of class struggle.

In retrospect, I feel that political movements in Mao's China were unbelievably absurd. According to Mao's formula, 5% of the total population were bound to be bad. Whether it was the Three-anti and Five-anti Campaigns, the Campaign to Suppress Counter-revolutionaries, or the Anti-Rightist Campaign, all used this formula to sort out targets. If you were unfortunately sorted into this 5%, then your life would be upended. Those severely punished would be executed, those lightly punished would be sent to labor camps, and the rest would be destined to lead a miserable life under tight control.

Some people today still consider Mao Zedong a great "national hero." By eliminating 5% of the population, he would remain a "wise ruler" for the other 95%. But 5% of the over half a billion people living under Mao's rule comes to over 30 million people, more than Europe's total casualties in WWII! As for those who sing Mao's praises today, they are mainly leftists or offspring of leftists, who have benefited from the persecution of millions.

After a few months in the Political Parties Division, I fully understood its functions: identifying trends, adjusting relationships, managing arrangements, and facilitating transformations. Our division's most frequent job was to summarize the words and actions of prominent figures of minor political parties in written reports for secretaries of provincial and municipal CCP committees. At that time, our department produced a biweekly classified newsletter called **Reports on Situations**, which was edited by the secretary of the Department Office and based on materials provided by other offices and divisions concerning United Front work and reactions to politics at the Party Central, provincial, and municipal levels. In the beginning, I was only in charge of its section on minor political parties. Later, since I was skilled at summarizing, I often took over the newsletter. In 1964, the "Four Cleanups Movement" got underway and the secretary of the Department Office was reassigned to this new assignment, while I took over all writing responsibilities for our department, including speechwriting for department leaders and participation in the drafting of provincial and municipal governments' work reports to the respective People's Congresses. I was extremely busy, sometimes having to work overtime late into the night, but I was young and energetic. When I got hungry working at night, I would go out to the yam vendor on our street and buy two roasted yams. Some coworkers called me a "text machine," fed by yams and producing endless texts.

As for "adjusting relationships" and "managing arrangements," they meant that officers of our division were often sent to various enterprises and institutions to persuade them to implement the Party's United Front policy and arrange for prominent figures in minor political parties to serve in some nominal leadership positions and be included in political delegations to the People's Congress and the PCC. "Facilitating transformations," on the other hand, referred to the policy of educating and transforming minor political parties, which was one of the Party's fundamental policies. We had to enforce this policy constantly in order to serve the political purpose of ensuring that minor political parties tamely "listen, follow, and stride" as the CCP's political tools. Every time I saw a prominent figure from one of the minor political parties speaking at the People's Congress or the PCC, I found it hilarious, because drafts of their speeches had been submitted to the UFWD the day before for review, and many sections had been entirely altered by me.

After the Anti-Rightist Campaign, the CCP Propaganda Department organized a theoretical discussion of whether "intellectuals should consciously serve as the Party's tame tools." The outcome of the discussion was of course affirmative. For a time, minor political parties also affirmed daily that they should serve as "tools." Therefore, every symposium that the UFWD held for the minor political parties was entirely devoted to high praise for the CCP, and everyone was encouraged to think and behave in unison.

This was surely one of the strangest instances of partisan politics in the history of the world. My descriptions above are a truthful depiction of the so-called "multi-party cooperation and political consultation system" that the CCP has been advocating and promoting as a "socialist party system with Chinese characters."

Chapter 6: Businesspeople Talking "Self-Transformation"

According to Mao Zedong's analysis of mainland China's class struggle status after the establishment of the communist regime in 1949, China's class relationships had changed fundamentally, and the primary domestic conflict had become that between the working class and the bourgeoisie. The CCP's policy toward the bourgeoisie was to enforce a socialist transformation via nationalization of private enterprises. In the essay On People's Democratic Dictatorship, published shortly after the preparatory meeting for the PCC in June 1949, Mao declared:

> *Such remolding of members of the reactionary classes can be accomplished only by a people's democratic dictatorship under the leadership of the Communist Party. When it is well done, China's major exploiting classes, the landlord class and the bureaucrat-bourgeoisie (the monopoly capitalist class), will be eliminated for good. There remain the national bourgeoisie; at the present stage, we can already do a good deal of suitable educational work with many of them. When the time comes to realize socialism, that is, to nationalize private enterprise, we shall carry the work of educating and remolding them a step further. The people have a powerful state apparatus in their hands—there is no need to fear rebellion by the national bourgeoisie.*

These words clearly demonstrated that the elimination of private ownership and of the bourgeoisie was the CCP's political goal. In fact, the CCP regime was very aggressive toward the industrial and commercial bourgeoisie. From the Three-anti and Five-anti Campaigns in 1952 to the Public-Private Partnership in 1956, the business sector was the main target of attacks. The end purpose of the policy to "ally with, educate, and transform" the national bourgeoisie was, in fact, to eliminate them.

After the industrial, commercial, and handcraft sectors' transformation via the Public-Private Partnership, the UFWD's at various levels focused on United Front work with business elites and established the Divisions of Business Sector Figures Work, commonly known as the Business Sector Division. In the UFWD of the Nanjing municipal CCP committee where I worked, the Business Sector Division had a director and two United Front officers who were all former underground CCP members in Nanjing as mentioned in Chapter 3.

As an aside, I remember one UFWD cadre who had worked for many years in the commercial sector and had maintained the habits of neat clothing and good manners cultivated in his line of work. His hair was always immaculate and his leather shoes always polished. Such habits were civilized behavior, but during the Cultural Revolution they were denounced as bourgeois, and he soon gave them up.

The Business Sector Division handled United Front work toward the China National Democratic Construction Association (CNDCA) and the All-China Federation of Industry and Commerce (ACFIC), commonly known as the "Two Organizations." Since the CNDCA was in essence a political party, its membership was voluntary. The ACFIC was formed to centrally organize all industrial and commercial businesses. All private businesses in the industrial and commercial sectors were required to register as members of the ACFIC. These two organizations were "the same workforce bearing two signboards" and shared a building in the city center that used to be a private mansion. The provincial and municipal branches of the other minor political parties were all in a four-story building behind the West Garden of the former Presidential Palace of the Republic of China.

Leadership of the CNDCA and the ACFIC mainly consisted of former bosses of large-scale industrial and commercial businesses with substantial capital. When the amount of capital was assessed during the implementation of the Public-Private Partnership, few businesses in the whole municipality had capital exceeding a million RMB. Jiangnan Cement Factory's capital was assessed to be three million RMB, and Yong'an Emporium at Fuzimiao just over one million RMB. The bosses of these two businesses both became municipal vice presidents of the "Two Organizations."

Interestingly, there were very obvious differences between the clothing worn by those from the industrial sector and those from the commercial sector. Industry figures were predominantly intellectuals who had received higher education, often abroad. They wore relatively modern clothes. Although few wore western suits, their tunic suits were still well made and the colors and materials adapted to seasonal changes. Among commerce figures, however, many still wore traditional robes. For example, Mr. Huang of Yong'an Emporium often wore silk robes and looked very much like the owner of a fabric store. Some young UFWD cadres and I joked that Mr. Huang could easily play the role of an evil landlord in a revolutionary opera.

Although business elites were the nominal leaders of the "Two Organizations," they were only political decorations and as useless as the ears of a deaf person. The real power belonged to CCP members sent by the UFWD. For example, the then secretary general of the municipal CNDCA committee was a former member of the underground CCP branch in the Central Emporium, whose CCP membership remained a secret after the communist takeover in order to facilitate his United Front work in the business sector. Among the national leadership of the "Two Organizations," the position of secretary general was also occupied by senior underground CCP members such as Sun Qimeng and Lu Xuzhang, who were among the famous "red capitalists." They were the true leaders of the "Two Organizations," and business people regarded them as Party delegates to whom they reported and from whom they sought directives. Every time local leaders of the "Two Organizations" traveled to Beijing to attend national committee conferences, they would come back to local meetings and recite the Party delegates' talks word for word, and businesspeople would treat these talks as if they were imperial decrees.

Employees of the "Two Organizations" were mainly transferred there from trade unions in factory and retail businesses. Most of them worked as factory workers or store apprentices before the communist takeover, and many were recruited by the CCP into the "Tiger Hunting Teams" during the Three-anti and Five-anti Campaigns and later the nationalization of private businesses. Their job was to denounce business owners, many of whom were reduced to kneeling and begging for mercy, while activists in the "Tiger Hunting Teams" were allowed to join the CCP on account of their high level of class awareness. It was an ingenious strategy to use these people to transform the bourgeoisie. They were nominally employees of the "Two Organizations" working for the organizations' leaders, but were actually representatives of the working class tasked with monitoring and transforming the latter. Many of them were not well-educated and often carried out actions considered compromising to the business elites in order to demonstrate their progressive thinking and their distance from the bourgeoisie. For example, some members of the support staff were supposed to deliver hot water in thermos bottles to the offices of organizational leaders but only delivered it to the secretary general's office, intentionally skipping the offices of the president and vice presidents, who were business elites in nominal leadership positions. The support staff members claimed that although these business elites had been served in the past, they should do some physical labor now and get hot water by themselves. Once, when the president and vice presidents told a support cadre to request cars from the sedan unit of the PCC, the cadre refused bluntly, claiming that "the secretary general didn't arrange for this, so I don't do it." Such incidents continued until the UFWD director general convened an all-hands meeting of CCP members in the United Front system and educated them on the policy of "respecting non-CCP figures to improve cooperation."

The UFWD had also tried to identify highly educated business elites as targets of enticement and cooptation. Underground UFWD cadres befriended these elites and offered them inducements in the form of notifications about upcoming political movements, financial assistance for their children's educational opportunities, etc. For example, Mr. Rong of Shanghai was favored in every political movement by the UFWD and was transformed from a leftist into a "red capitalist," finally joining the CCP.

Like Mr. Rong, Mr. Chen of Nanjing also became a target of cultivation. He was formerly a managerial talent loyal to capitalists, had a college degree, worked on engineering and technical jobs, and rose up to become the general manager of a privately owned cement plant before the communist takeover. Due to his extensive social connections, he was an active figure in the business sector. Shortly after the communist takeover, KMT spies in Nanjing considered him usable, tried to entice him to join their underground anti-communist network, sent agents to contact him several times, and issued him a small handgun for self-defense. However, Mr. Chen had figured out that the tide had already turned against the KMT. Not wanting to risk his life for a lost cause, he voluntarily reported the espionage activities to the Public Safety Bureau and assisted them in exposing a spy network, several members of which were later executed. Because of his meritorious actions, he was highly appreciated by the then municipal CCP committee secretary, Ke Qingshi, who directed the UFWD to publicize him as a role model for progressive democratic figures. Mr. Chen also had very good communication skills and knew how to defer to the CCP in all political matters. A skilled dancer and tennis player, he often fraternized with the mayor and the CCP committee secretary. He therefore had very good political fortunes, serving as a non-CCP vice mayor for a time and retiring from the post of vice chairperson of the provincial PCC.

The UFWD also used Mr. Chen to learn about the mindset of business elites. A frequent ploy of his was to invite business leaders of the "Two Organizations" to dinner at a restaurant (the bill would actually be paid by one of the businessmen), where he encouraged them to drink and enticed them to speak freely, later reporting their words to the UFWD. I remember he once informed us that the greatest wish of business elites was that the CCP would ease its policies and engage in "three harmonies and one meagerness" internationally (meaning to develop and maintain harmonious relations with the West, the Soviet Union, and neighboring countries, and provide meager aids to poor and insignificant countries). In addition, they hoped the CCP would follow a policy of "three individuals and one fixing" domestically (that is, encouraging plots for individual use, free markets run by individuals, enterprises with individual responsibility for their own profit or loss, and fixing output quotas on a household basis).

At the time, I was tasked with editing the department briefings once or twice a week, and finding these words very representative, I produced a special briefing titled *Heartfelt Words of the Bourgeoisie*. The content of this briefing was soon submitted to the CCP Central Committee via the central UFWD's classified briefing, which was only accessible to leadership of the Central Secretariat and Politburo. After reading it, Mao Zedong wrote instructions on the document that "three harmonies and one meagerness" and "three individuals and one fixing" were the political platform of capitalist restoration and should be treated as a new form of class struggle. This became one of the justifications for Mao's strong emphasis at the CCP's Tenth Plenary Session of the Eighth Central Committee on "talking class struggles every day, every month, and every year." Chen Yi's talk shortly before about "removing labels and bestowing crowns" on intellectuals at the Intellectuals Work Conference in Guangzhou was interpreted as a right-leaning talk. Soon newspaper editorials appeared denouncing the "trend of individual farming" and the "trend of verdict reversal," and reaffirming "never to forget class struggles." The CCP lost credibility concerning its United Front policies, and some people complained that "the Party's policies are like the moon, changing every day." A businessman remarked in private that the Party's treatment of non-CCP figures and intellectuals was similar to making dough, adding some flour when it is too wet and adding water when it is too dry, until it is ready for baking.

Some business people cared little about politics before the communist takeover, and were completely focused on doing business and making profits, regardless of which party happened to be in power. After the Public-Private Partnership, they lost control of all capital, and their business know-how became useless. Instead, they were turned into political puppets who were made to talk at big and small meetings, constantly saying they must "listen, follow, and stride" and testifying to the transformation of their minds. Many couldn't adapt. For example, a textile tycoon of the province began as a street vendor and grew his business step by step into a giant enterprise with four or five textile factories by the time of the Public-Private Partnership. His assessed capital in the Partnership was 30 million RMB, exceeding the famous Rong family in Shanghai by 10 million (because the Rong enterprise had split into three). He was assigned to the highest position among businesspeople in this province and always sat on the rostrum in sessions of the National People's Congress. However, he felt uneasy with the political constraints placed on him by the CCP. At a biweekly symposium of minor political parties held by the UFWD, he suddenly let slip some heartfelt words:

> *I was born a businessman, and I still dream of doing business now. When I started my factories, in order to learn from foreign businesses, I went to the*

US, pretended to be an apprentice, and worked in a US factory to observe their technologies and learn some skills secretly. Later, my identity was leaked by someone, and the factory's foreman found me and ordered a few henchmen to beat me up before kicking me out. Now the CCP wants me to be an official, and I feel it is really to be an official for the CCP because it is not necessary to spend money or use your brain. My job is simply to come to the office to read some documents and then affix my seal to them. I arrive every day on time and leave after affixing my seal and signing my name, with a chauffeur taking me to and from the office.

His words triggered a roar of laughter in the meeting room. Afterwards, I summarized his words into a briefing, retaining as much of his personal speaking style as possible. The secretary of the provincial CCP committee read this briefing and highly praised it for vividly depicting a senior capitalist's true colors. For this, I received commendation from the department director general and was jokingly called a "briefing expert" by coworkers.

The CCP took a carrot-and-stick approach toward business figures. Alternating aspects of this tactics rendered business people submissive. As early as in the Three-anti and Five-anti Campaigns, business people started to get a taste of the CCP's ferocity. Back then, a mobilization conference for the campaign was held in the municipal People's Hall (formerly the National Great Hall, where the National Constituent Assembly and the First National Assembly of the Republic of China took place), which had over three thousand seats. The host and keynote speaker was municipal CCP committee secretary Ke Qingshi, who emphasized the seriousness of illegal business activities and singled out two businessmen on the spot. One of them was a builder who was accused of cutting corners and compromising safety when building airfield runways for the air force. The other was a pharmacist accused of selling counterfeit drugs to Chinese troops in the Korean War, resulting in soldiers dying of infections. Once the accusations were made, the attendees demanded harsh punishment of counterrevolutionary profiteers. Policemen dragged the two businessmen from their seats to the stage, while people shouted, "Shoot them! Shoot them!" The two were immediately tied up by several soldiers, sent to the execution ground, and put in front of a firing squad. This all happened within several minutes and the two suspects had no chance to say a word in their own defense. Businesspeople among the attendees had never witnessed this kind of terror and were scared out of their wits. They were told to confess any wrongdoings. Some of them immediately turned over their life savings to the government, while some even committed suicide. After this round of intimidation, by the time of the Public-Private Partnership the surviving business people had all turned over their capital and property to the CCP. Many business elites accepted the reality of the times and spoke always of "self-transformation," not knowing when they themselves would become targets of persecution.

As for the so-called petty bourgeoisie at the bottom of the business sector, they were in dire straits. When the Public-Private Partnership was implemented in the municipality, fewer than 7,000 people were labeled as belonging to the industrial and commercial classes, whereas over 10,000 people were labeled small business owners. The latter became second-class citizens because they were not significant enough to become targets of United Front work and were not part of the nominally ruling proletariat-turned-working-class either. Most of them were absorbed as waged laborers into mid-to-large-scale Public-Private Partnership enterprises at the municipal or district level, but being out of favor, they were discriminated against everywhere. In every political movement, the CCP committee or workplace branch would refer to them as opponents in class struggle, and their children would be negatively affected in educational advancement, job placement, military recruitment, and CCP and CYL membership applications. Few of these people would go through the Cultural Revolution unscathed.

For example, the husband of a nationally renowned actress of the Yue Opera was the owner of a small store before the communist takeover. He was labeled a member of the small business owner class, and assigned to the Xinhua bookstore as a counter assistant. His wife was so popular that the UFWD arranged for her to become a delegate to the National People's Congress, and after each session of the Congress she would meet with Premier Zhou Enlai, who was known to be especially attentive to actresses and female stars and often invited them to his office to dine and chat. These actresses all considered it a high honor to meet with Premier Zhou, and would report the encounter to the UFWD as major good news after they returned home. Once Zhou asked if this actress had become a CCP member, and she explained that the secretary of her opera troupe's CCP branch considered her husband politically discredited and recommended that she distance herself from her husband for the sake of her own reputation. Some even suggested she divorce her husband and remarry. However, this actress believed she should stand by her husband in bad time and she maintained a harmonious marriage despite significant political disadvantages. However, despite her noble sentiments she could not withstand the denunciations of her by Red Guards and Rebels during the Cultural Revolution and committed suicide by stabbing herself with a pocket knife. That day, several young cadres of the UFWD, including me, rushed to her home and saw that she had already been carried onto the ambulance, while her home was covered with blood. For several days I had no appetite. Her beautiful and noble image still resides in my heart, and I pray that her soul has found eternal peace in heaven.

Perhaps the young generation in China today will have a hard time understanding how the label "capitalist" was such a burden to so many people, who were forced to exist in a political shadow and even lost their lives because of it. Karl Marx said, "*capital comes dripping from head to foot, from every pore, with blood and dirt.*" This curse condemned the Chinese people to decades of hardship. The elimination of private ownership that the **Communist Manifesto** advocated led to the construction of the massive edifice of communism using the skulls and bones of capitalists, in one of the great tragedies of human history.

In the early 1960s, as a result of the famine caused by the Great Leap Forward, many Chinese starved to death in rural areas and food supplies in urban areas were very limited. Out of consideration for some prominent figures outside the CCP, the UFWD issued each minor party cadre of director level and above a pound of cooking oil, a pound of meat, a pound of eggs, and sometimes half a pound of milk every month beyond their regular rations. Some business elites had previously given up the fixed interest from their capital in the Public-Private Partnership to demonstrate their progressiveness, and the UFWD notified them individually that they could begin receiving fixed interest payment again to improve their families' lives. These business figures were very grateful for this opportunity to reclaim their due incomes.

During this period, the UFWD hosted banquets catered by the Café of the PCC in the small dining hall at the West Garden after each biweekly symposium in order to provide prominent democratic figures the opportunities to eat good food. The invitees to the banquets were local leaders of minor political parties and the Federation of Industry and Commerce, but UFWD cadres like myself who attended the symposiums along with department leaders could sometimes partake of the great meals. Many times, secretaries of provincial and municipal CCP committees also joined us, and I believe it was because even these high officials couldn't easily throw lavish banquets under the conditions at the time. When the Party secretaries attended a banquet, liquor was usually served. The Office of the PCC particularly requested the transfer of an excellent chef from the Trade Union Federation's café in order to improve the cuisine. This chef's surname was Xu, and we called him Big Old Xu. He used to be a senior chef in a Yangzhou cuisine restaurant, whose signature dishes were fish head and tofu stew in clay pot and braised meatballs in brown sauce. He would serve these two dishes in person and introduce the banquet course. He was always complimented by the guests on his culinary skills, and then Big Old Xu's face would light up with joy.

Unfortunately, Big Old Xu came under Party attack during the Cultural Revolution. The Rebels accused him of being a capitalist because of his involvement in a restaurant joint venture many years previous. He was labeled a loyal lackey of the bourgeoisie after receiving praise from minor political party leaders. Big Old Xu was furious, saying that he was an authentic member of the working class because he worked at the Trade Union Federation. He had obeyed the Party Organization's assignment and transferred to the PCC to continue his revolutionary work, so it was a grave injustice to label him a capitalist.

Chapter 7: The So-Called "Organization Department of CCP Outsiders"

Some democratic figures referred to the UFWD as the "Organization Department of Party Outsiders." This name could be understood in two ways. On the positive side, it appeared democratic figures had their own Organization Department and were organized just like CCP cadres. Some "leftist" democratic figures even called the UFWD their "maternal home." On the flip side, the so-called "Organization Department" made democratic figures as submissive as CCP cadres, without any political liberties.

In fact, the tasks of the UFWD in plain terms were "investigation, management, arrangement, and control" of democratic figures outside the Party. One of the tasks, elaborated on in earlier chapters, was to make political arrangements of Party outsiders. Before fulfilling this task, it would be necessary to thoroughly and completely find out each democratic figure's political history and current state of mind, which was called "investigation and examination." This was equivalent to the "cadre investigation" procedure carried out by personnel organs, whose regular management functions such as promotion, demotion, transfer, and disciplinary action, were also performed by the UFWD with regard to democratic figures. As to the implementation of the policy of "allying with, educating, and transforming" intellectuals, it was outright brainwashing, and should rightly be considered a form of mind control.

The UFWD had its own personnel units. The central UFWD had a Personnel Bureau, and provincial and municipal UFWDs had personnel divisions. These units were not only in charge of the personnel issues of the UFWD and its subsidiaries, but also in charge of the investigation and personnel arrangement of United Front work targets such as intellectuals and business people. Municipal-level targets of United Front work mainly consisted of the following: minor political parties and the Federation of Industry and Commerce's municipal committee members; municipal People's Congress delegates and PCC members outside the CCP; professors of higher education institutions; industrial enterprises' engineering directors and above; and hospital's deputy chief doctors and above. Since many people were involved, the Personnel Division of the municipal UFWD drafted a list of names of nearly a thousand people based on previous years' records. The records of those who had actual jobs in non-political institutions and enterprises were managed by their employers' personnel organs, and the remainder (including full-time committee members of minor political parties, full-time members of the standing committee of the municipal People's Congress, in-house members of the municipal PCC, and members of the municipal Board of Advisors) were all managed by the UFWD's Personnel Division directly.

After the communist takeover in 1949, from the Campaign to Suppress Counterrevolutionaries in 1950-1951 to the Campaign to Weed out Hidden Counterrevolutionaries in 1955 and the Anti-Rightist Campaign in 1957, all Party and government organs, enterprises, institutions, schools, and hospitals, etc., in mainland China carried out large-scale internal campaigns to investigate and examine cadres. Their personnel units set up dedicated Cadre Examination Offices and assigned some CCP-member cadres to carry out internal examinations and investigations of particular targets. Significant resources were spent investigating cadres under special suspicion, whose families and social relationships were thoroughly investigated. The UFWD was not an exception. Its Cadre Examination Office was nominally subordinated to the Personnel Division and not only examined cadres of the UFWD, the PCC, minor political parties, and the Federation of Industry and Commerce, but also examined non-partisan figures in the municipality. At the time, other offices reassigned cadres to assist with external investigations. When I worked at the Ministry of Interior in Beijing before transferring to the UFWD, I was also reassigned to the ministry's Cadre Examination Office for over a year and dispatched to many locations in Northeast China to conduct investigations.

I recall that a section-level cadre in the ministry was investigated because one of his friends and classmates who went to Hong Kong after the communist takeover wrote a few letters to him, and he didn't report such correspondence to the Party Organization. The fruitless investigation involved over ten institutions, while he didn't even know he was being investigated. Interestingly, this individual became the director general of the Cadre Examination Bureau of the Ministry of Civil Affairs after the Cultural Revolution and helped me to get redress for the injustice I suffered during the Cultural Revolution. Such bizarre cases of mutual investigations were fairly common in the history of the CCP.

When I transferred to the UFWD in 1961, large-scale internal campaigns to investigate and examine cadres and weed out hidden counterrevolutionaries were on the way out. It could be said that nearly all targets of United Front work in the municipality had been investigated, and only some very complicated cases were still under investigation. Sometimes, the Personnel Division temporarily borrowed a few cadres from other offices to help with personnel work because it was short-handed with only three full-time officers. Officers of the Political Parties Division helped with the investigations of intellectuals and prominent figures of minor political parties, and from the records of intellectuals outside the Party, I learned that some of them had formerly served sentences in labor camps and were released early in the 1950s because of the need for industrial development. For example, when the CCP assumed control of military factories such as the aircraft plant and telecommunication equipment plant in Nanjing after the communist takeover, several senior engineering staff were condemned to labor camps as counterrevolutionaries because they had once had high military ranks awarded by the Defense Ministry of the KMT government. Later, they were sent back to the factories and received sentence reductions and releases because the CCP urgently needed technical experts to develop its military industry. Having been at death's door and continuing to find themselves targets of United Front work, they had ample reason to dread the CCP.

The chief engineer of a factory making military telephones had a Ph.D. degree from the US and taught in the Department of Electrical Engineering of Tsinghua University for eight years before transferring to the military industry near the end of WWII. Since he was a colonel in the KMT military, he was considered an historical counter-revolutionary and was sentenced to twenty years of hard labor in an agricultural labor camp in northern Jiangsu Province. In 1953, the CCP discovered that he was an exceptional expert on the military industry and released him after reexamination and assigned him to the chief engineer position of a large military factory with over 2,000 employees. After his imprisonment, he feared the CCP so much that he would address every cadre he met as "leading cadre" and always spoke submissively. Later, he would serve as a member of the standing committee of the municipal PCC. Every time I visited him on official business, he stood up respectfully and would not sit down until I asked him to. Evidently he saw no difference between CCP cadres and the wardens of the labor camp, whom he didn't dare to offend. Once, I visited his home to deliver the certificate of election to the standing committee of the PCC and found a gray-haired man with thick spectacles in a study full of technical books in foreign languages, whose demeanor expressed profound respect and humility. Thinking back on his this once proud academic with a degree from America, an undisputed expert in his field, I felt a hard-to-describe sadness. This was the tragedy of a generation of Chinese intellectual elites.

There were quite a few technical experts in Nanjing, including the chief engineers of the radar factory (China's first), the plane factory, the tank factory, and the biggest wireless communication equipment factory in China. At the same time that they made great contributions to the development of China's military industry, they stood accused of being cultivated by the KMT and "American imperialists." They tolerated insults and continued to work hard without knowing that their records contained expressions such as "spy suspect with serious historical problems" and "use under control." These so-called conclusions of cadre examinations would accompany them to the grave. They were like second-class prisoners in a military concentration camp who would never be promoted to a higher rank.

Some democratic figures who were previously targets of United Front work had their fortunes upended after cadre examination. For example, Mr. Kang, who was formerly one of the leaders of the local Federation of Industry and Commerce and had always taken progressive stands after the communist takeover, was accused of uttering so-called rightist words before the Anti-Rightist Campaign, and it was found out during cadre examination that he had been a member of a peripheral organization of the KMT's military intelligence apparatus. As a result, his past and present transgressions were counted together, and he was sentenced as a historical counterrevolutionary to fifteen years in a labor camp, where he died.

The UFWD's cadre examination of targets of United Front work was very strict and would "investigate history going back three generations." Special emphasis was put on overseas relationships.

Overseas mail correspondence with individuals of unclear identities could become a cause for suspicion and have political impact. I recall the examination of a democratic figure who joined the CDL before the communist takeover. He had always been progressive politically and applied for CCP membership, but when his history was investigated, it was found that he formerly had a girlfriend when he attended high school in Hong Kong, and this lady later went to Taiwan and married a government official there. He confessed that shortly after the communist takeover of the mainland, this former girlfriend sent him many letters from Hong Kong. It turned out the contents were nothing but declarations of love and how much she missed him. Although he reported this relationship to the CCP without any reservations, the CCP still suspected he was a spy left behind by the KMT, and committed a large amount of resources to doing internal and external investigations of him. His girlfriend's family background in Hong Kong was investigated by the Hong Kong Bureau of the Xinhua News Agency. Although no incriminating evidence was turned up by the investigation, because the ex-girlfriend was now the wife of a KMT government official, the suspicion could never be cleared and was always hanging over him, preventing membership in the CCP and keeping him at a low political level without any opportunity to get an important position. I heard that not until the late 1980s, shortly before his retirement, was he admitted into the CCP and promoted from division level to bureau level. Tragically, this individual probably never realized that his political career was severely compromised by a passing love affair in his youth.

Another important function of the Personnel Division was to arrange for political positions ("personnel arrangement"), such as who should serve as delegates to the People's Congress or as members of the PCC, who should become the presidents or vice-presidents of minor political parties' local branches, and who should be assigned to deputy positions in the government such as vice mayor or deputy director general of municipal government bureaus. The procedure for making such arrangements was mainly the following: First, the working meeting of the municipal CCP committee or the directors general would determine the guidelines of the personnel arrangement, such as needing a representative of the intellectual community, a female, or an ethnic minority. Next, the Personnel Division would come up with a list of names containing the primary and backup candidates' names and resumes. Finally, this list of names would be submitted to the UFWD director general, and the final nominee would be selected by the working meeting of directors general following discussion. Some high-level positions such as vice mayor required approval by the municipal CCP committee secretary. As for elections in the People's Congress and the OCC, they were mere formalities. No wonder some members of the standing committee of the People's Congress liked to joke that there was a division of labor for elections (the Chinese word for "elect" literally consists of two characters meaning "select" and "raise", respectively): The Organization Department and the UFWD were to "select" and People's Congress members only needed to "raise" their hands.

The Personnel Division of the UFWD kept detailed records of political arrangements of United Front work targets going back to the establishment of the communist regime, which were classified and inaccessible to regular cadres.

Experienced personnel cadres were needed to make personnel arrangements. When I was at the UFWD, the director position of the Personnel Division changed hands several times, but a section-level United Front officer who started working at the UFWD shortly after the communist takeover never changed his position, like a veteran minister who served a succession of emperors in ancient times. He was extremely familiar with people's backgrounds and could elaborate on the history of specific figures without reading their records. He became indispensable to the department leadership on personnel arrangement issues, to the extent that even though the director of the Personnel Division could sometimes take a leave of absence when personnel arrangements were discussed in the department's working meeting, it was absolutely necessary that this officer be present. If he was away on a business trip, the department leadership would have the office staff call him or send him a telegraph asking him to return and attend the meeting.

In addition, he was a necessary fixture at the Chinese New Year's Eve celebration every year. It had become a tradition when I worked at the UFWD for the provincial and municipal CCP committees and governments to hold a New Year's celebration banquet, usually at Nanjing Hotel on Zhongshan Road, which was administrated by the Foreign Affairs Division and was the only hotel authorized to host foreign guests. There were usually eighty to ninety tables at the banquet, attended by such prominent figures as delegates to the National People's Congress, members of the standing committees of the provincial and municipal People's Congresses, minor political parties' local presidents and vice presidents, provincial and municipal government officials at director general level or above, and secretaries and vice secretaries of provincial and municipal CCP committees. Because of the large number of high-ranking attendees, the seating arrangements became the most important matter. Improper arrangement of seats or incorrect sequence of names in news reports were treated as a serious political incident. Therefore, the preparations before the event had to be very thorough. Generally, the secretary of the provincial CCP committee should be the first to appear, followed by the governor, the lieutenant governor, those from National People's Congress, national PCC, provincial People's Congress, provincial PCC, municipal People's Congress, municipal PCC, etc. This sequence should never be altered. As to seating, the host table must be seated by secretaries of provincial and municipal CCP committees, the governor, the mayor, the chairpersons of provincial and municipal People's Assemblies and PCCs, and some of their deputies. To sort out the sequence of appearances and the seating was the job of an expert. The indispensable officer of the UFWD Personnel Division was such an expert, and he kept personal records of previous attendee sequences as if they were more important than CCP central committee documents. Sequence sorting became his exclusive domain, and the sequences he came up with were usually approved by the department director general with hardly a glance.

Every year when this banquet was held, in order to help attendees get to their seats quickly and without any hitches, the UFWD always asked its young cadres to moonlight as ushers. On this day, we would get dressed up, arrive at the banquet hall at 4 to 5 pm, line up on the two sides, and wait. The banquet seating would usually start at 6:30, and we would lead the lower ranking guests to their seats first. Leaders on the host table would arrive at about 7:00, entering the hall in the preset sequence with welcoming music playing, while lower-ranking guests would stand up and applaud. Then the secretary of the provincial CCP committee would give a New Year's address, after which the banquet would start.

As a young cadre, I served as an usher every year at the celebration and couldn't have New Year's Eve dinner with my family at home. We would usually wait until about 8 pm, an hour after the banquet had started, to have our New Year's Eve dinner in a small hall, where three or four tables would be set up for the service staff. Actually, we would be served the same food as at the banquet and the chefs often gave us bigger portions and extra drinks, including Maotai and whiskey, which were quite rare at the time. Although I ate very well at the New Year's Eve celebrations, I always felt uneasy because I wasn't with my family. To please my parents, once the event ended at the Nanjing Hotel, I always went to my parents' home and had longans and lotus seed soup to signify the union of the extended family. By this time, my daughter would have fallen asleep on the sofa and we would wake her up and carry her back home. Fortunately, my home was only a twenty-minute walk from my parents'. Once, it had snowed heavily, and my wife and I repeated the old saying that a fall of seasonable snow gives promise of a fruitful year. We decided to bring our daughter to Xuanwu Lake the next day to take some photos in the snow. I am reminded of this heartwarming scene every New Year's Eve, and each time I feel like going back to that moment, walking home at night in the snow. Now I am a wanderer far from my homeland and don't know whether I will ever retrace my steps along that dreamlike road in Nanjing.

After the banquet ended at 8:30 pm, it was customary to have a dance party in the big guest hall. To liven up the ball, not only was the local military band invited to play music, but also female dancers from art and cultural institutions including Jiangsu Song and Dance Ensemble and Nanjing Song and Dance Ensemble were invited to dance with the leaders.

Actually, many high-level CCP officials were fond of ballroom dancing mainly because, at the time, dance was the only entertainment besides movies. In addition, Mao Zedong and other leaders of the Party Central frequently threw dance parties and their inferiors followed suit. When I worked at the Ministry of Interior of the central government after graduating from college, the then minister Zeng Shan (father of Zeng Qinghong) and deputy minister Mr. Zhang were both crazy about dancing. Zhang had an artificial leg after his calf was amputated during the war, but when he danced, no one could tell he was handicapped. Since I was the secretary of the

CYL general branch in the Ministry of Interior, and since dance parties were always organized by the League Organization, I actively participated by inviting bands—the Ministry of Interior having its own band of the blind that was of excellent quality—arranging for tickets, inviting female teachers from kindergartens and elementary schools, and laying out the ballroom. In the process, I also became an avid dancer.

Twice, deputy minister Zhang was given a ticket to a dance party at the International Club but couldn't go because of a conflict of schedule, so he gave the ticket to me and arranged for a chauffeur to drive me there. At the International Club, I once saw Premier Zhou Enlai, who mostly danced a foxtrot. Witnessing his graceful dancing and his lively conversations with young women, I lost my sense of mystery and awe regarding central leaders. As for some high officials using their power to sexually prey on women at dances, this is one of the dark sides of man's nature. We can only guess whether Mao engaged in such behavior, but it would have been quite surprising, given his unchecked power and the fact that he was often surrounded by beautiful women, if he had indeed remained chaste. Given that throughout history powerful leaders have always had many women, it should not surprise us that Mao did the same.

One deputy director general of the provincial UFWD had a lot of seniority, having joined the CCP in 1925. He was a little bookish and didn't like to dance, but for the sake of work relationships, he often sat in the ballroom for about an hour and chatted with some members of the leadership before leaving. His wife was a cadre who used to be a member of a guerrilla unit in northern Jiangsu Province. She had a candid personality and frankly expressed her opposition to dances, saying, "Why dance? To meet some beautiful girls and select concubines." I laughed and said jokingly, "You should keep a close watch on your husband and not let those young beauties entice him." She said, "Even if it crossed his mind, he wouldn't have the courage to do it." We both laughed hysterically. Such elderly couples who respected each other at all times were truly rare among high-level CCP officials. The ethics he learned from reading Chinese classics were probably a greater constraint on him than the Party Charter. I admired this couple very much and considered them good friends despite the difference in our ages. Unfortunately, they were persecuted severely during the Cultural Revolution, and the wife attempted suicide one night by jumping into a pond. After the Cultural Revolution, the deputy director general had his position restored and his wife lived into her eighties and died peacefully.

Another important task of the Personnel Division was to choose candidates for the *lianghui* (People's Congress and PCC). To this day, the CCP's propaganda organ continues to proclaim that "the institution of the People's Congress is democratic politics with socialist characteristics." It refers to it as a "fusion of powers," and claims it is the most democratic institution in the world. This "fusion of powers" theory was borrowed from Soviet constitutional theorists. The Soviet Union enacted a constitution in 1936 (often nicknamed the "Stalin constitution") and celebrated it as the most sophisticated constitution in the history of mankind. One of its elements, fusion of powers, distinguished it from the constitutions of capitalist states. Actually, the Communist Party of the Soviet Union made a farce of constitutional democracy. It is well known that a constitution is a political contract between a country's people and their government that guarantees the people's rights and limits the government's powers. If a constitution becomes the declaration of a monarch or a political party, can it still be called a constitution? It can only be the fig leaf of personal or one-party despotism.

The Communist Party of the Soviet Union dissolved over 20 years ago, and the theory of "fusion of powers" is no longer even a laughingstock of communism. However, such a political joke is still being repeated in China as if it were the truth, and canonical Marxist jurists still maintain that the institution of the People's Congress is a higher level of democracy than the parliamentary democracy in the West. Lately, a so-called theorist from the Central Party School of the CCP even claimed that there were three forms of democratic institutions in the world: first, Western parliamentary democracy, or electoral democracy; second, collective democracy under elite rule, or oligarchical decisional democracy; and third, consultative democracy, which was the road of democratic politics that the CCP was taking. Such a categorization is absurd. Legitimizing despotism as "decisional democracy" and "consultative democracy" is like the sugar coating on the vaccine pills for kindergarteners, but the Chinese people are not so easily fooled.

Today, CCP-controlled media maintain that the people's delegates are elected via democratic procedures which enable the people to fully exercise their democratic rights. Such lies are not even believed by the delegates. The procedure for choosing people's delegates and members of the PCC is actually the fabrication of these "political dolls" which the UFWD participates in. Nothing could be more obvious.

People's delegates and PCC members are jointly picked by the CCP's Organization Department and the UFWD, commonly known as the Two Departments. Their division of labor is such that People's delegates and PCC members who are CCP members are nominated by the Organization Department, while those outside the CCP are nominated by the UFWD. Before each election of the *lianghui*, the provincial and municipal Party secretaries in charge of personnel affairs will work together with the directors general of their corresponding Two Departments to determine the compositional ratio of seat allocations. Usually, local levels may appropriately adjust the general guidelines from the CCP central committee (e.g., minority ethnic regions should have more minority seats). When I worked in the UFWD, the guidelines were roughly 70% CCP members and 30% Party outsiders (including members of minor political parties and those without party affiliations). Then the ratios of genders and sectors are considered (e.g., women, intellectuals, workers and peasants should each have no fewer than 10% of seats). Sector ratios can be adjusted based on current conditions (e.g., when industrial development is on the rise, the representation of science and technology professionals should rise). As for model workers of industry and agriculture, many of them are local Party cadres, such as CCP branch secretaries of villages representing agricultural workers and secretaries of factories representing industrial workers.

After the ratio guidelines are settled, the personnel divisions of the Two Departments will produce preliminary candidate lists to be discussed and modified by department meetings. These lists are then submitted to the local CCP committee, where they will be finalized by the working meeting of the standing committee. Afterwards, the lists will be submitted to the *lianghui* for the formal procedure of elections. The candidate lists are already fixed by the time they reach the *lianghui*, like manufactured and packaged dolls waiting only to be displayed in showcases.

After such internal processing, the final lists of *lianghui* candidates are mainly composed of high- and low-level officials. The proportion of CCP members is almost always higher than what is recommended in the general guidelines, because some semi-retired senior cadres need these positions. As for delegates to the National People's Congress and members of the National PCC, their candidate lists are determined by the Two Departments of the CCP central committee and sent down to the provincial-level People's Congress and PCC. In order to avoid the embarrassment of some candidates not being elected to the national level by the provincial *lianghui* (for which the Two Departments' leadership would be held accountable), CCP members among the *lianghui* delegates and members convene in a temporary Party committee meeting on the night of the preparatory conference before the official opening of the *lianghui*. The election of national candidates is declared a Party imperative, and anyone who dared to cast a nay vote would face political consequences. Since CCP members are the majority of the *lianghui* delegates or members, it is guaranteed that the national candidates on the official list will be elected.

The actual process for producing delegates and members of the *lianghui*, as described above, is a "democratic" procedure with unique Chinese characteristics. As a result, the *lianghui* have become conferences of leading cadres at various levels. Many delegates and members of the *lianghui* wear new suits, the women are usually beautifully dressed, and some ethnic minorities even dress like actors on the stage. It is very much like a festival, with delegates and members flattering each other and singing the praises of the CCP. Some seize the opportunity to network and make backdoor deals, scrambling for power and fortune. All of this is in sharp contrast to the intense debates and voting in parliaments of democratic countries. Meanwhile, the CCP media have the audacity to claim that the "socialist democracy" in China is much better than Western democracy.

A hilarious incident occurred in 1963 at the plenary session of the Nanjing municipal PCC. When the secretary of the municipal CCP committee listened to the report on preparations before the meeting, it occurred to him that all the vice chairs of the municipal PCC were leaders of minor political parties, none of whom was an engineering or technical professional. In order to motivate engineering and technical professionals, the PCC should add a senior non-CCP representative of this group to its vice chairpersons. After the UFWD received this directive, it held a meeting and finally decided that Mr. Shi, the chief engineer of the largest machining tool factory in the municipality, was an appropriate candidate. The UFWD then visited Mr. Shi at his home to notify him. He happily accepted this new arrangement as it demonstrated the CCP committee's trust in him. Because of the UFWD's advance notification, Mr. Shi arrived at the meeting hall of the PCC on the day before the meeting started, preparing to assume his new title. However, PCC cadres at the entrance didn't know of the UFWD's plans to add a new vice chairperson and assumed that Mr. Shi had come to the wrong meeting hall and patiently explained to him that this was the meeting hall of the PCC, not the People's Congress. Embarrassed, Mr. Shi stood at the entrance for half an hour until the director general of the UFWD arrived and took him in.

In the meeting, Mr. Shi went through three rounds of voting, first on his membership in the PCC (as he was not a member previously), then on his membership in the standing committee of the PCC (as only standing committee members could serve as vice chairpersons), and finally to elect him as a vice chairperson of the PCC. The then acting chair of the PCC declared that the voting should be done via applause, and Mr. Shi was propelled to the position of vice chair by three rounds of applauses. A PCC member from the business sector observed with irony that it was unnecessary to have three rounds of applause, and just one round should be sufficient. In this way, the policy of "greater, faster, better, and more economical" could be implemented in voting. This triggered a lot of laughter. It is no wonder that many people describe the *lianghui* in the following jingle: "People's delegates raise their hands, PCC members clap their hands, and parties follow the Party's magic wands." This is a vivid characterization of "socialist democracy" in China.

Since membership in the *lianghui* is a political reward, some non-CCP figures who are keen on social status and reputation try their best to express their loyalty to and sing high praises of the Party during the *lianghui*, so that CCP committee leaders will safeguard their positions or assign them to better ones. Non-CCP figures know clearly what the CCP wants to hear. If they dared to express any critical opinions, they would find themselves uninvited to the next meeting or lose their *lianghui* membership after their current term expires. Those with a strong desire for fame and fortune poke their noses into every corner to seek the position of People's Congress delegate or PCC member. One of my friends, a law professor with a selfish personality who didn't get along well with colleagues, applied many times for CCP membership but was always denied by the local CCP branch. Later, he realized he stood a better chance of getting ahead if he joined one of the minor political parties. He became a member of the provincial PCC and later became a member of the national PCC. At that point he told me with arrogance: "Now that I have more or less joined the upper class, let's see, would the local CCP branch's petty leaders dare treat me poorly?"

Of course, there are some intellectuals and engineering and technical professionals who focus on their jobs and are not interested in politics. They don't pay much attention to political developments and feel it is a waste of time to attend political meetings. Once I met an architect who was the vice president of the local architectural engineering school. When she was chosen by the UFWD to become a delegate to the National People's Congress, a deputy director general and I were dispatched to deliver the certificate of election to her. She was quite surprised and indicated she knew nothing about the matter and hadn't participated in the election. She jokingly said, "I sat at home, and a certificate came from heaven. I find it difficult to accept such a big assignment."

Chapter 8: On the Stage and behind the Scenes of *Lianghui*

At the local level, the *lianghui* is also a PR show for Party and government leadership, who boast about how good local conditions are, taking this opportunity to exhort the local masses to "Love the Nation, Love the Party, and Love Socialism."

Usually, the national *lianghui* are held in March, after the Chinese New Year, whereas the local *lianghui* take place earlier, in January or February. When the Chinese New Year is late on the western calendar, the local *lianghui* may be held right after it, when most people are still on the Chinese New Year break. The local *lianghui* can't be held at the same time as the national *lianghui* because local Party and government heads are mostly also delegates to the National People's Congress, and local PCC leaders are mostly national PCC members, who are expected to attend both the local and national *lianghui*. The UFWD, as the CCP committee's specific operational organ working on the *lianghui*, is almost completely devoted to *lianghui*-related work for more than a month. The UFWD is one of the directors behind the scenes of this political spectacle. It directs the performances on the stage based on a screenplay written by the CCP committee. Therefore, the success of the *lianghui* is a measure of the competence of the UFWD and its leadership, and no UFWD cadre dares to take it lightly. Every cadre is nervous during the *lianghui*, right up to the final moments.

The UFWD's participation in the *lianghui* work can generally be divided into four stages:

First, the drafting of the government work report. This report is a summary of the government's work during the past year and an outline of next year's goals. At the national level, the government work report is equivalent to the US president's state of the union address. The CCP government uses this report to make the Party Central's policies and achievements known to the people. It can be considered the general guidelines of the following year's policies and the blueprint for all sectors and all institutional work. Therefore, the report must be extremely well written, and those cadres who excel in writing can take advantage of this opportunity to shine.

When I worked in the Nanjing CCP committee UFWD, the *lianghui* work lasted from mid-December to mid-January. It began with the UFWD's cadre mobilization meeting. Cadres of all offices, including secretaries and typists, were mobilized to focus on preparation for the *lianghui*. During this period, no one could take a leave of absence without special circumstances. The highlight of the preparation was to participate in the drafting of a government work report, commonly done by a writing team consisting of secretaries of the municipal CCP committee office and the UFWD. I participated in the drafting of nearly ten government work reports, and the chief writer was always Mr. Shen, associate chief secretary of the municipal CCP committee office, who was assisted by two or three junior secretaries.

The drafting of this report had to go through several gates. First, the working meeting of the municipal CCP committee decides its basic tone, known as the "primary foundation." This established the main theme, or central idea, of the report based on the Party Central's directives and local work specifics. For example, the report in 1962 was based on the Party Central's policy to "adjust relationships, summarize experiences, strengthen solidarity, and mobilize intellectuals" and reflected the CCP's new tactics after its Conference of Seven Thousand. I recall that Mr. Peng, the municipal CCP committee secretary in charge of our work, gave the directive that "achievements must be sufficiently stated, and shortcomings must also be stated pertaining to the truth." When our several writers had a meeting to digest his words, one of the writers asked: "Can it be understood as stating all the shortcomings clearly?" Mr. Shen, the chief writer who chaired the discussion, immediately explained that this interpretation was wrong, and shortcomings should be considered only one digit among ten. We all laughed. After the meeting, I said to the writer who asked the question, "If the report was really written as you proposed, we would probably all end up in the Wawaqiao detention house." He asked: "Is this so severe?" I said that the secretary's directive should only be interpreted with the difference between insiders and outsiders in mind. If too many shortcomings were written into the report, we would be blamed and punished. My colleague seemed to agree.

Not surprisingly, the tone of the government work report in 1963 made a U-turn, after Mao suddenly began talking a lot about class struggle at the CCP's Tenth Plenary Conference of the Eighth Central Committee. He emphasized that focusing on class struggle would be effective in the short term, which quickly put a damper on the political atmosphere. Mao mentioned class struggle in ideology and denounced "three harmonies and one meagerness" and "three individuals and one fixing," which were actually the so-called new trends in class struggle that we provided in our briefings (see Chapter 6). Those non-CCP figures who expressed complaints in the *lianghui* in 1962 about the great famine caused by the CCP's Great Leap Forward began to fear that they would be labeled as rightists against the "Three Red Flags" if another Anti-Rightist Campaign were to take place. No wonder non-CCP figures said privately that the Party's policies were like the moon, changing every day.

The main goal of the government work report in the *lianghui* was to proclaim the CCP's great achievements to the people. This involved the repackaging of the CCP's self-claimed "greatness, glory, and correctness," supported by specific statistics and examples. Words such as "fundamentally" and "greatly" appeared numerous times throughout the report. Compulsory education was "fundamentally" universalized, and the people's health care was "fundamentally" improved. Apparently, conditions were not just good but great.

When the "socialist moral education" of the people was discussed, several role models were usually provided. This was called "raising role models to learn from, catch up with, and surpass." I remember that when suggesting role models of exemplary customer service, we used Miss Yu for three consecutive years. She was a sales assistant who wasn't highly educated but was very polite and amiable. Because of wildly flattering reports by the media, she was called a "living Lei Feng" (Lei Feng was a role model who had died) and it was arranged for her to become a member of the provincial PCC. By our third report, we all felt her accomplishments were too familiar and that repeating them was not appropriate, but we failed to find any other role model in the commerce sector. Since delegates and members of the *lianghui* raised the people's grievances about the bureaucratic behavior of the service sectors, we had no choice but to use her once again as a role model. This young lady in her early twenties told me privately that she hoped this would be the last time she would be made a role model, because she had been invited by many businesses to give speeches on "socialist commerce morality," causing her to be absent from work frequently, and her coworkers didn't like her because they had to cover for her. I deeply sympathized with this young lady's position but could only console her by reminding her of the Party's cause.

After the government work report was drafted, it was still necessary to hold a formal meeting of the standing committee of the municipal CCP committee to discuss and approve the report. Then it had to be approved at the municipal government meeting, chaired by the mayor and attended by heads of all departments and bureaus, before it could be considered official. Afterwards, it was reviewed in the standing committee meetings of the *lianghui* and finally submitted to the People's Congress.

Another form of preparation performed by the UFWD before the *lianghui* is to participate in the review and gatekeeping of the work reports of the standing committees of the *lianghui* and the speeches of non-CCP delegates and members of the *lianghui*.

The work reports of the People's Congress and the PCC must strictly follow the guidelines laid out in the government work report. Since these two reports are auxiliary and don't receive much attention, the UFWD mainly takes care of their proofreading and political gatekeeping, and they are generally drafted by the secretaries of the People's Congress and the PCC, only to be reviewed by the UFWD. They mainly offer a "day-to-day account" of the *lianghui* proceedings and outline the next year's goals. In the work summary portion, the principle of talking more about achievements and less about shortcomings is also followed. This norm is repeated year after year, only differing in specific examples. A secretary who has worked in the People's Congress or the PCC for many years can very easily draft the reports following the formula. Therefore, the UFWD has little to do but gatekeep the wording and politics of the reports. Usually, this is done after the government work report is essentially finalized.

Another task of the UFWD is to review the speeches of non-CCP delegates and members of the *lianghui*, quite a demanding task. When I worked at the UFWD, we were required to guarantee the unanimous approval of the government work report in the *lianghui*. It was also necessary for non-CCP democratic figures to give speeches and express their views following the basic tone of the government work report. Praises of the "great achievements" of the government from the mouths of outsiders formed a political chorus at the *lianghui*. To preempt the negative political impact of any delegate or member's "friendly fire," it was necessary to review and control the manuscripts of their speeches. The operational procedure generally involved three steps:

First, through cadres of minor political parties and the Federation of Industry and Commerce or liaison officers of the *lianghui*, the UFWD established the main topics of their speeches, usually educational funding, teachers' compensation, investment in medical facilities, public sanitation, urban transportation, housing, and work conditions and worker benefits. Liaison officers produce written transcripts of their conversations and submitted them to UFWD officers. The UFWD's purpose was to communicate with *lianghui* speakers via the liaisons. The main theme of speeches must be to sing praises of the Party's "Greatness, Glory, and Correctness." Any criticism must be slight and not compromise the Party or the government. Some suggestions for improvement were permissible in order to demonstrate the democratic spirit of the *lianghui*.

Second, those leaders of minor political parties who had participated in the *lianghui* many times were already very familiar with the UFWD's methods of controlling speeches, and some of them even submitted manuscripts of speeches to the UFWD well in advance in order to solicit suggestions. If they had no objections to the contents of speeches, UFWD officers would return the manuscripts and say that there was no need to review them (when actually the manuscripts had been thoroughly vetted). If some contents were considered controversial, the UFWD would communicate its disapproval through the leftist cadres of the minor parties in order to make it appear that the UFWD didn't directly censor the manuscripts. Since so many speeches were delivered at the *lianghui*, reviewing manuscripts was an enormous burden for UFWD officers, and if we couldn't finish during working hours, we would take manuscripts home to read. Manuscripts were reviewed very carefully, since any mistake could lead to reprisal. Apart from correcting grammar mistakes, the purpose of the review was mainly to do political gatekeeping and not to improve the language. Nevertheless, most speeches followed the Party's formula, such as citing Chairman Mao and using expressions taken from Party Central documents. As a result, some delegates and members would be so bored while listening to the speeches that they would doze off.

After the proofs of *lianghui* speech manuscripts were printed, UFWD officers would participate in the proofreading, and if obvious errors were found, they could hold off the printing of manuscripts and send someone to communicate with the would-be speaker. If the communication wasn't successful, the manuscript would be reduced to an outline so that inappropriate content could be removed. During the general conferences of the *lianghui*, the scheduled speech would be replaced with a written statement, citing lack of time as the excuse. The would-be speaker would be told that there was too little time to print the full manuscript so it had to be summarized in the form of a written statement.

Another important task of the UFWD during the *lianghui* was what was called in the 1960s "grasping trends in classes struggles." A dedicated "briefing team" was set up during *lianghui* sessions in charge of writing meeting briefings. There were two types of briefings, one of which was open to the public, printed, distributed to all members and delegates, and used by the media as an important reference. These briefings were summaries of group discussions and talks by provincial and municipal leaders in small group discussions. Usually, they were edited and printed during the night and distributed in small group meetings the next morning. Another type of briefing was internal, prepared by the UFWD, and only distributed to standing committee members of the provincial and municipal CCP committees and leaders of the UFWD as special issues of the UFWD's **Situation Briefing**. Since I was the editor of the UFWD's regular briefing, I naturally participated in this function during the *lianghui*. Source materials for briefings were submitted by cadres of minor political parties, the Federation of Industry and Commerce, and Party members among *lianghui* members and delegates. This became the main reference for the Party to grasp trends in the *lianghui*. The CCP's monitoring and spying were everywhere. Some non-CCP figures who were unfamiliar with the workings of the *lianghui* were unaware that private conversations could be collected in briefings and have serious consequences.

At this point, I can't help but recall a friend of mine who had just become a professor of law over twenty years ago. He was very ambitious and soon became a member of the PCC. He said, "Now I have the right to freedom of speech." At the time, I felt like warning him: "Your words and actions are all monitored, and your big mouth could get you into big trouble." Sure enough, he spoke too much during the 1989 pro-democracy movement and was purged from the PCC during the next selection.

The UFWD must guarantee the success of "elections in the *lianghui*." Although the personnel arrangements are pre-determined by the Organization Department and the UFWD, they still have to pass the votes in *lianghui* conferences. If it is a general election, ballots must be cast procedurally in the conference halls. To avoid misgivings about the candidates, a high voter turnout was required. Therefore, the night before voting, the temporary Party committees of the *lianghui* would hold Party member meetings to declare that it was imperative that candidates get high numbers of votes and that every Party member participating in the *lianghui* commit to casting a yeah vote. Although Party members constituted 75-80% of *lianghui* delegates and members, provincial and municipal Party leaders still had to ensure a high voter turnout to avert any mistrust of new government leaders. In previous years, some Party-member delegates and members of the *lianghui* would often leave the conferences to go back home for private matters or to visit friends and relatives, causing the attendance rate to drop to 70% or lower. To avert a low rate of attendance on the day of voting, provincial and municipal Party secretaries would announce in Party member meetings that those who were absent from voting without pre-authorization justified by special circumstances would be treated as violators of Party discipline and face punishment. As for supporting cadres of the *lianghui* like myself, we stayed all the way till the end. The last briefing was usually about comments on newly elected leaders, consisting mainly of praise, and some entertainment. Throughout the *lianghui*, I had to leave home early and return late. I did overtime work at home and was sometimes so busy I had no time to eat, let alone go home to see my wife and kids. I often hoped the *lianghui* would end sooner so that I could go home and get a good sleep.

Finally, one thing worth noting is the logistics of the *lianghui*. Citing leadership's words, it is necessary for delegates and members to eat well, drink well, and stay well, so the *lianghui* budget is a considerable outlay every year. In the nearly ten *lianghui* that I participated in, delegates' and members' meals were budgeted at 20

RMB per person per day, which was equal to over half a month's wages of a worker at the time, when a Level 3 technician only earned 38 RMB a month. Together with board and transportation, each attendant spent about 50 RMB a day, approximately 600 RMB for the duration of the *lianghui*. The entire budget of the municipal *lianghui* was about 2 million RMB, equal to about 200 million RMB today. It is said that the national *lianghui*'s spending is now in the area of 280 million RMB, and the spending in all of China probably exceeds 20 billion RMB.

Even in 1962 during the national economic crisis, over a dozen dishes were served on the dining tables of the *lianghui*, and the final banquet after the closing ceremony was even more luxurious. Each night, I collected some leftover dishes to take home to my parents and kids. My mother always hated to finish the foods right away and saved them over a few days. At the time, when I saw thin and malnourished beggars from northern Jiangsu Province and northern Anhui Province on the streets, I always thought of Du Fu's poem: "*Wines and foods gone bad are rotting – the crimson doors behind; There are corpses, people frozen to death, at the wayside!*" To entertain *lianghui* delegates and members, there were also art and opera performances every night, including some performed by famous actors with national awards. However, lower cadres like myself had to write briefings and didn't have any chance to watch the performances.

Later, after I became a legal scholar and witnessed my colleagues praising the institution of the People's Congress, I always felt disgusted. Although the legal textbooks of communist China copied from the Soviet Union's "unity government" theory that claimed that "the Soviet was the highest level of parliamentary democracy," the Soviet Union didn't bother to create the disguises that China did. The CCP regime, in order to produce a political show for non-CCP figures to advocate for "socialist democracy", designed a "bird cage" called *lianghui* for intellectuals to perform in. Many non-CCP figures are self-intoxicated in this "bird cage" where there is delicious food to eat, performances to watch, and limousines to ride in. The people, on the other hand, are increasingly appalled by this expensive political show. I wonder what those *lianghui* delegates and members would feel after learning its insider stories and whether they could avoid being ashamed of themselves.

Chapter 9: Routine Jobs of the Political Consultative Conference

According to some experts on the CCP's history, the historical origin of the Chinese People's Political Consultative Conference should be traced to the National Political Participation Conference (NPPC) in Chongqing during WWII, which was established during the wartime alliance between the KMT and the CCP. At the time, because the CCP and some democratic figures strongly advocated constitutional democracy in China and opposed the KMT's one-party rule, the KMT made a political compromise and agreed to form a National Political Participation Conference consisting of members of the KMT, the CCP, and minor political parties. Seven CCP members—Mao Zedong, Lin Boqu, Wu Yuzhang, Qin Bangxian, Dong Biwu, Chen Shaoyu, and Deng Yingchao—were appointed NPPC members. This was the earliest political consultative institution in China.

After the victory of WWII, to avoid a civil war the KMT and the CCP signed the October 10 Pact in 1945 and agreed to establish the Political Consultative Conference, which was convened in Chongqing in January 1946. It consisted of 38 delegates: eight from the KMT, seven from the CCP, nine from the Democratic League, five from the Chinese Youth Party, and nine non-partisan figures. CCP delegates included Zhou Enlai, Dong Biwu, Wang Ruofei, Wu Yuzhang, Ye Jianying, Lu Dingyi, and Deng Yingchao. Later, due to the civil war, this conference was dissolved without notice. CCP historians refer to it now as the "old PCC."

In September 1949, the Chinese People's Political Consultative Conference was convened in Beijing. Now known as the "new PCC," this conference enacted the "Common Principles" as the basis for the formation of the central government of the People's Republic of China (PRC). The PCC served as a provisional legislature until the National People's Congress was convened in 1954, which enacted the PRC's constitution. After that, the PCC was maintained as the organizational form of the United Front in order to exhibit the "institution of political consultation with multi-party cooperation" as an important element of "socialist democracy."

Before the Anti-Rightist Campaign of 1957, some minor political parties in the PCC suggested that the PCC should be elevated to the "upper house" and the People's Congress be redefined as the "lower house," following the bicameral system in the West. This was completely contrary to Mao's vision of a one-party despotic dictatorship. Although Mao elaborated that the CCP and the minor political parties should "coexist for the long term and monitor each other," he also emphasized that intellectuals were part of the bourgeoisie and must undergo a complete transformation of their thinking. In fact, Mao's true intention was to use the PCC as the equivalent of the Hanlin Academy in the imperial era, where prominent scholar-gentlemen were given a stipend. Therefore, those who suggested that the PCC should become the upper house of the parliament were labeled "rightists" and ended in disgrace. Even Luo Longji, a leading supporter of the CCP in the old PCC who fought the KMT tirelessly, was labeled an ultra-rightist and died a miserable death.

The PCC Became Non-CCP Figures' Workshop of Mind Transformation

The PCC's organizational structure at provincial and municipal levels was an office led by a full-time vice chairperson who was usually a semi-retired former CCP secretary, governor, or mayor. Other vice chairpersons from minor political parties were mostly nominal. A secretary-general and several vice secretaries general handled day-to-day work. The PCC office had a Division of Secretariat, a Division of Personnel, and a Division of Administration, just like a government organ. Its officers were full-time permanent employees with compensation packages at various levels. When I first joined the UFWD, the provincial and municipal PCCs shared the same office in the former Presidential Palace of the Republic of China. Later, the provincial and municipal PCCs separated into different offices, with over 70 or 80 employees, including chauffeurs.

Among the PCC members, many were non-CCP figures and intellectuals in various professions, including full-time officers of minor political parties. A small number of PCC members had no other real jobs and were referred to as in-house members. These were mainly former military and administrative officers of the KMT (including KMT defectors and former prisoners of war who had been pardoned, many of whom were generals), former National Assembly members and Legislative Yuan members, and senior democratic figures who had helped the CCP before the communist takeover. These members generally numbered over twenty, constituting less than ten percent of the PCC. They were handled by the Personnel Division of the PCC and paid by the PCC directly.

In addition, there were two institutions effectively administrated by the PCC: the Office of Advisors and the Institute of Culture and History. The Office of Advisors was a United Front institution nominally reporting to the government. The title of advisor was in name only and was given to senior democratic figures, including those KMT military and administrative officers who had defected to the CCP. It appeared to be an advisory institution of the government but was actually an institution of honorary titleholders. Its administration and personnel arrangements were handled by the PCC's Secretariat Division. For a period, the director of the provincial Office of Advisors was Luo Qingchang, who was formerly vice secretary general of the State Council in Beijing and was demoted to this position after being renounced in the State Council's Anti-Rightist Campaign. Since he did underground work with Zhou Enlai for a long time and participated in negotiations between the KMT and the CCP as a member of the CCP Delegation, he liked to say jokingly that, "coming to Nanjing is to revisit a formerly familiar place, except that I lived in a small villa in New Meiyuan Village (i.e. the office of the CCP Delegation) last time and never entered the Presidential Palace back then, where my office is located now. This has really been a major change of fortune from one end to the other."

As for the Institute of Culture and History, it was also a largely inactive institution to which the CCP assigned some community leaders and democratic figures. The three guidelines of assignment were "old, cultural, and impoverished." "Old" meant over 60 years old. "Cultural" meant some special abilities in literature, art, history, or philosophy, usually with experience in cultural institutions such as the National Institution of Translation or the Central Academy of Fine Arts during the KMT era. Some members of this institute had helped the CCP's underground work before the communist takeover and hence were specially favored. For example, Mr. Song was a secretary of the county commissioner of Liling County, Hunan Province in the 1920s when Song Shilun, a leader of the communist guerillas, was captured by paramilitary forces there and sentenced to death. Being a relative of Song Shilun, Mr. Song successfully lobbied to have Song Shilun released on bail for reasons of young age and naivety. Song Shilun later joined the Red Army and became a lieutenant general after the establishment of the communist regime. To pay the debt of gratitude for Mr. Song's saving his life, he personally took Mr. Song from his rural home in Hunan to Nanjing to become a member of the Institute of Culture and History with a stipend of 100 RMB per month, so that Mr. Song could enjoy his remaining years in comfort.

The Institute of Culture and History in Nanjing had seventy to eighty members at its peak, and the entire PCC system there consisted of nearly three hundred people. On every festive occasion, PCC members and employees held celebrations in its meeting hall, packed with over five hundred people, including family members. The then PCC secretary general, Mr. Tang, was very interested in culture and entertainment and often organized young employees to perform on the stage. In the New Year's celebration of 1965, he spoke to me several times and persuaded me to join one of the performances. I recall that it was a one-act drama encouraging youth to join the military, and I played a young soldier. I borrowed a military uniform and performed on the stage like a professional actor. This was the only time I ever performed on stage in my life, and I received quite a bit of applause. Many people said to me afterwards that they hadn't anticipated a nerdy "writer" could perform so well.

After the Anti-Rightist Campaign of 1957, democratic figures in the PCC all realized how ferocious the CCP could be. They all knew the saying "a loose tongue can get you into trouble," and they swore loyalty to the CCP and talked a lot about transforming their minds at PCC meetings. The leadership of the PCC, in order to turn the PCC into a workshop of mind transformation for non-CCP figures, established a Committee of Studies as one of the working committees. Pre-existing committees included the Committee of Culture, Education and Sanitation, the Committee of Legal Systems, and the Committee of Finance and Economy. The name of this new committee didn't clearly specify the meaning of "studies." In the beginning, some democratic figures suggested it should be named "Committee of Marxism-Leninism and Maoism Studies." However, many thought this name was not only too long but also not precise, because the scope of studies should be broad, and Mao Zedong

90

himself had said that we should learn from the working class and the peasants. Finally, the name "Committee of Studies" was adopted, which was rather ambiguous but more inclusive.

Of the many committees of the PCC, many were only used for propaganda purposes in the media. For example, when a sanitation campaign was carried out, the Committee of Culture, Education and Sanitation would be convened for demonstration effect. Otherwise it would convene only once or twice a year. On the contrary, the newly formed Committee of Studies, although seemingly out of place, became the PCC's most tightly organized and most frequently convened substantive committee.

The PCC's Committee of Studies was chaired by a full-time vice chairperson of the PCC, and all other important leaders of minor political parties were arranged to be this committee's vice chairpersons, e.g., business figure Mr. Liu, who was also one of the deputy governors, and Mr. Wu from the culture and education sector. Members of the Committee of Studies included in-house members of the PCC, members of the Office of Advisors, and presidents, vice presidents, and secretaries general of minor political parties, almost covering all the non-CCP figures in the PCC system. In addition, the committee was divided into seven or eight big groups with vice chairpersons of the committee as group leaders and full-time leading cadres of the minor political parties (mostly the secretaries general) as assistant group leaders. Each big group was further divided into several small groups, such as the Small Group of Office of Advisors and the Small Group of the Institute of Culture and History. Altogether, there were over two hundred members.

The Committee of Studies established an extensive study plan and employed three full-time cadres to lead instruction. Groups convened Monday, Wednesday, and Friday afternoons and a weekly meeting was held to discuss takeaways from the studies. Such an intensive program gave the appearance of a university education. It could be said that the UFWD was the "office of student affairs" and that non-CCP figures were being held as academic captives. In a way, it was amusing to see the "students"—many of whom were prominent figures during the KMT era—taking notes, listening to lectures and joining in discussions like well-disciplined middle school students. A former major-general of the KMT who defected to the CCP and was made a deputy director general of the municipal Bureau of Transportation always rode a bicycle to classes even when it was raining. Once it rained so hard that his clothes were all wet, and I said to him: "Mr. Jia, you could have asked the bureau to dispatch a car for you." He said with a smile, "One has to be reborn to transform one's mind. Riding a bike in the wind and rain is not only an exercise but can also touch one's soul." I thought to myself: "How prestigious he was when he commanded tens of thousands of troops! The moment he surrendered his troops to the CCP, could he have ever imagined that he would live like this now?" The CCP had transformed these former KMT military commanders into school children with no hope of ever graduating.

In every small group of the Committee of Studies there was a full-time transcriber to record attendance and take notes. They were mostly full-time employees of the PCC or the minor political parties who not only kept records of the meetings but also observed the thoughts and opinions of figures from different sectors as reflected through their studies. Some of this information was considered indicative of trends in class struggle and was collected by UFWD writers like myself, who would select some of the information and write briefings for municipal and provincial CCP leaders.

During the PCC's study activities, municipal and provincial CCP leaders and directors general of the propaganda departments were often invited to give "political addresses," mainly to extol the merits of industry and agriculture and present positive role models. Such addresses were pre-arranged in the "plan of studies." For example, from 1963 to 1964, the Committee of Studies proposed to provide instruction about the "three isms," i.e., patriotism, internationalism, and socialism. For the topic of patriotism, an army commander who participated in the Sino-Indian War was invited to give an address. On the topic of internationalism, a model worker from Norman Bethune Medical University was invited to speak. Concerning socialism, model workers spoke on the subject of "recalling one's sufferings in the old era and contrasting them with the happiness in the new era."

Once, a model worker from the agriculture sector was invited to speak. He was a low-level cadre in a commune and formerly a peasant. During his address, he talked about his work as a long-term hired hand for a landlord in the old era, saying that on holidays and festivals the landlord would treat his employees with a good meal with meat and wine. Since their family members couldn't eat meat often, they would take some leftovers home. Hearing this, people felt that the landlord's employees were eating better than the rationed three ounces of meat per month. The speaker later put aside the draft of his speech and began to talk about the Great Leap Forward that resulted in a great famine. The topic became a critique of the man-made famine and the CCP's arbitrary orders. Later, the office director of the Committee of Studies was strongly criticized by the UFWD director general, who blamed him for not reviewing the draft of the address carefully.

The Committee of Studies was also in charge of arranging for leaders of minor political parties and the Federation of Industry and Commerce to attend biweekly meetings hosted by the UFWD. Municipal and provincial CCP secretaries in charge of United Front work were often invited to talk at these "situation briefing meetings." When the "Four Clean-ups Campaign" was carried out in 1964, the meeting was dedicated to the briefing about the Party Central's policy on the campaign. Talks by the Party secretaries at these meetings were transcribed by the UFWD and conveyed to all members of the minor political parties and the Federation of Industry and Commerce.

Making the PCC a Giant School of Maoism

In 1964 and later, following Lin Biao's "Studying *Selected Works of Mao Zedong*" campaign in the military academies, a campaign of "Creatively Studying and Using Maoism" was carried out throughout the nation. The PCC's Committee of Studies organized many conferences on "teaching and using Maoism" and invited worker role models, peasants, and soldiers who excelled in studying *Selected Works of Mao Zedong*. One speaker who left a strong impression was an old lady named Gu Atao from the rural area of Wuxi. (After the Lin Biao Incident, we learned that she was promoted by Lin's wife, Ye Qun.) Although illiterate, this old woman speaking in her local dialect was very eloquent and could fluently recite the "three old essays" of Mao. In order to "recall one's sufferings in the old era and contrast them with the happiness in the new era," she used a range of local proverbs and received applause from the intellectual audience, who felt like they were listening to the talk show of Wang Shaotang, a famous entertainer in Yangzhou. The more talks she gave, the more popular she became, and she became a "political star" on the national stage. After the Cultural Revolution began, she become a delegate to the National People's Congress and one of the vice chairpersons of the municipal and provincial Revolutionary Committees. However, her good fortune didn't last long. At the height of her popularity, the Lin Biao Incident occurred and she suddenly lost favor. After the Cultural Revolution ended, this miserable peasant woman in her seventies was looked down upon everywhere and had to work as a popsicle vendor on the streets of her hometown to make ends meet.

At the time, in response to Mao's directive that "all the nation should learn from the People's Liberation Army," the PCC instructed all members of the Committee of Studies to watch the drama Sentinels under Neon Lights, played by the Ensemble of the Political Department of Nanjing Military Region, and arranged for them to visit the role-model military units to learn from the "Good Eighth Company on Nanjing Road." Many members of the PCC swore loyalty to the Party, saying they would "absorb Maoism into their soul and blood." Something hilarious happened when they visited a "role model" militia unit in a rural area to watch target practice and share takeaways from their studies of *Selected Works of Mao Zedong*. The militia unit's stories were narrated by the militia director of the local township, an uneducated veteran injured in the Korean War. During his narration, he said: "Every militia member of our township follows Chairman Mao's exhortation to learn from the Old Eighth Route Army on Nanjing Road, in that we wear straw sandals instead of leather shoes and use makeshift facial cream in clam shells instead of vanishing cream." The audience suddenly burst into laughter because the director had mistakenly said "Old Eighth Route Army" instead of "Good Eighth Company." A director general of a minor political party came forward to cover up the mistake, saying: "The term is different, but the spirit is the same, because the commander of the Good Eighth Company in the drama is an old Eighth Route Army member." We did our best to hold back our laughter.

Inspired by these so-called "teaching and using Maoism" events, a leftist member of the PCC wanted to show his progress in politics and asked permission to give an address to the whole conference of the PCC in an annual *lianghui* with the title "Turn the PCC into a Giant School of Maoism." This request was reported to the UFWD director general, who considered such a title too far-left, which would compromise the PCC's position as a United Front organization, contradict Party Central directives, and have a negative influence on PCC members. UFWD officers were immediately dispatched and the title was changed to "Takeaways from Maoism Studies." In a spirit of self-transformation, the speaker uttered a lot of nonsense but nevertheless avoided any further political embarrassment.

At the time, there was a popular catchphrase that went like this: "The KMT had many taxes; the CCP has many meetings." We all had a toolbox for coping with continual meetings. After going through many political movements, everyone knew the principle that "a loose tongue can get you into trouble." Some believed that they were safe as long as they stayed silent, and in every meeting they would say that they needed to transform themselves but never express their opinions. Some would read an excerpt of an official document and end their talk by indicating their firm support and determination to carry it out. Some would keep their eyes closed and finally say a few words such as "I was educated by other people's talks and will study hard." Others liked to talk about irrelevant historical experiences and kept denouncing the old regime. Of course, some would say too much. As noted in Chapter 6, one time a business figure was talking about his experiences and said that he was born to do business and would sometimes dream of doing business, causing the whole room to roar with laughter. His words were considered as revealing the reactionary thoughts of the bourgeoisie who wanted to restore capitalism and were written into the UFWD's internal briefing and submitted to provincial and municipal CCP leadership as an example of a new trend in class struggle.

Another important daily task of the PCC was to organize PCC members and non-CCP figures to inspect grassroots work units. These so-called inspections were actually tours. Usually there were two major inspections every year, one in April and the other in September. Additionally, so-called "professional inspections" were conducted sporadically, similar to the inspections of compulsory education in elementary and middle schools and the sanitation and vaccination inspections organized by the Committee of Culture, Education and Sanitation.

The specific arrangements for transportation, touring, and accommodations were handled by the secretariat and administrative divisions of the PCC, while the thoughts expressed at these events were recorded by the UFWD as political trends. Therefore, officers of the UFWD usually made a point of participating in these activities in order to directly collect first-hand material.

To do this job well, the UFWD and PCC secretariat would send cadres half a month in advance to the UFWD of the districts or counties where the chosen targets of inspection were located. Such targets were usually "exemplary units" or "model units" and were required to accept the hosting of inspectors as a political task and guarantee "good introduction, good arrangements, and good accommodations." Meal menus and transportation arrangements had to be made well in advance. At the time, a PCC secretary named Jiang was an expert on such arrangements. Every trip was nominally led by a vice chairperson or the secretary general but was actually organized by Mr. Jiang, who we called an "inspection expert." Before each departure, people had to make sure he was on board and the driver couldn't start the coach until he gave the directive.

I recall that agricultural inspections were always performed in October Commune (also known as "October Red Flower Commune") because this commune was inspected by Chairman Mao in person. It was formerly called Qixia Commune and was renamed to commemorate Mao's inspection of it one October. The true story of the so-called inspection by Mao was that in late October 1961, Mao came to Nanjing for an inspection and stayed in a small villa near the Sun Yat-sen Mausoleum. One afternoon, seeing the beautiful autumn scene, he felt like going for a walk, and asked Jiangsu Province CCP committee secretary Jiang Weiqing to point out some nearby ancient temples. Jiang suggested Qixia Temple, which was about one hour's drive away. Mao asked if this was where Li Xiangjun attempted suicide as mentioned in the Qing Dynasty musical play The Peach Blossom Fan, and Jiang said it was, so Mao decided to visit it. Since the route passed by fields belonging to Qixia Commune, provincial leaders arranged for banners and slogans along the road and asked the commune's leaders to organize paramilitary members to disguise as peasants in the field for security. When Mao's motorcade passed by, he saw well-grown vegetables and some greenhouses beside the road (suburban agricultural land was mainly used to grow vegetables) and demanded a stop here on a whim for an inspection of the agricultural field. The director general of the Public Safety Department, who drove the leading car, immediately called up the commune's chief and

CCP branch secretary to brief Mao about the commune's population, crop yields, etc. While listening, Mao walked a few dozen steps in the field and also took a look inside a greenhouse, and the photo journalist accompanying Mao took photos of Mao talking with peasants. Mao left after less than half an hour for Qixia Temple, where he chatted with the presiding monk and appreciated the fall foliage, altogether spending three hours in the area. Half a month after Mao left Jiangsu, *Xinhua Daily* reported Mao's inspection of Qixia Commune on its front page and printed a large photo of Mao there. The commune then held a ceremony of celebration and changed its name to October Commune.

The Commune became a mecca for visitors, and many officials came here ostensibly to visit a model commune with the real purpose of touring Qixia Mountain and Qixia Temple. Because of the increasing number of visitors, the commune invested money in a large café in front of the temple named the "Maple Leaf Café" that could host about five hundred people. The project also created several full-time positions for tour guides, whose scripts were drafted with the aid of newspaper journalists. The CCP secretary of this commune could recite the script very well without referring to the printout, as if enumerating his family valuables. To satisfy PCC members and non-CCP figures, when many PCC members visited the commune two master chefs from the city were temporarily assigned to cook their famous dishes for lunch. Given the fact that food supplies in China were very limited at the time and meat had to be rationed, this lunch with several meat and fish dishes prepared by master chefs was more enjoyable than a New Year's feast. The visitors undoubtedly left with the impression that, no matter how persuasive the commune's propaganda was, it was less appealing than the tasty meal. We privately joked with a commune cadre that "it is materialistic to believe that one has to eat well before talking well." The cadre nodded and said, "Municipal leaders, please don't worry; we guarantee everything will be satisfactory. If anything was not done well, rural cadres like us would not get by." We all laughed.

These tourist visits were an inconvenience to the local peasants. In the small town where the commune was located, people would be mobilized three days in advance to do a major cleanup. No litter or open trash containers were allowed, and every household had to clean the sidewalks in front of their homes very thoroughly and put up signs welcoming PCC members. Every commune member was notified that if visitors asked any questions, answers must be in positive and never negative terms. If anyone spoke recklessly or made any trouble, there would be grave political consequences. To add more authenticity to the display, PCC members could spend an hour visiting peasants' homes after lunch. I recall that PCC members formed several small teams to visit peasants' homes separately, and they saw a lot of hams, salted meat, and dried chickens hanging below the eaves of every home. One PCC member couldn't believe it was possible for every household to have so much meat so long before the New Year's celebration, so he took a ham down for a closer look and saw a sticker with "Jinhua Ham for export." This PCC member asked the head of the household if these hams came from his own pigs. The commune cadre accompanying the visitors rushed to explain that this was cured meat made by this household for the Export Corporation. His explanation was so clumsy that everyone was embarrassed, and we could do nothing but smile at each other. No wonder there was a popular saying about such political deception: "Villages cheat the township, townships cheat the county, one level cheats the next, all the way till the State Council." We will never know the extent to which Mao Zedong was himself deluded by ploys such as these.

Another daily task of the PCC was to organize its members and Culture and History Institute members to write memoirs as historical materials. This originated from a proposal by Premier Zhou Enlai at a PCC conference in 1960. Zhou announced at this conference that non-CCP figures in the PCC had abundant historical experiences and should write them down truthfully to be preserved. There were to be no restraints on opinions or writing style, but the memoirs must stay true to historical facts. Later, the PCC established a Committee of Cultural and Historical Materials with full-time staffers. Actually, many in-house PCC members and Culture and History Institute members were former military and political figures of the KMT regime who had been pardoned by the CCP, while others had been denounced for involvement in various political movements. They were all very cautious in their writing and avoided any inappropriate words that might cause them to be accused of incomplete transformation or of extolling the former reactionary ruling class. They usually described the KMT military as highly corrupt and the CCP military as extremely competent, regardless of historical facts. I recall that a lieutenant general of the KMT military who had killed many Japanese invaders in the Battle of Taierzhuang during WWII and who was captured by the CCP in Tianjin during the Chinese Civil War initially described the KMT as very incompetent and corrupt. A deputy director general of the UFWD had a talk with him, saying that writing down historical materials was completely different from mind transformation and that the CCP would never denounce him for writing the truth. He went back to his job and produced a completely different memoir. However, two years later the Cultural Revolution began, his materials were interpreted as reactionary thought with the intent of restoring the old regime, and he was denounced so harshly that he almost died.

Nevertheless, the Committee of Cultural and Historical Materials managed to have over twenty books published before the Cultural Revolution, some of which were partly reviewed by writers of the UFWD. These historical materials partly preserved some historical facts, such as the achievements of the KMT military on the frontal battlefields in WWII, and became highly valuable records for later research on the war.

Chapter 10: Using Privacy to Control Prominent Figures

The UFWD not only openly carried out political and ideological education of its targets outside the Party, using the PCC as the organizational means, but also had secret methods of controlling their thoughts and behaviors. This was done by secretly probing their privacy to achieve the goal of turning these figures into "tame tools" of the Party who would docilely obey political orders.

It is well known that Chinese intellectuals were often more afraid of losing face than losing their lives. When their honors were in jeopardy, they might choose to save face regardless of political integrity. Since China was a deeply conservative society until recently, whenever a sex scandal occurred, the involved parties would be ruined, with nowhere to hide from public opinion. As early as the KMT era, when the CCP carried out underground operations, its United Front organ already used private information as a means of coercing some non-CCP figures into following CCP orders. A prominent member of the KMT, who later joined the RCCK, was a womanizer and had a sweetheart who was an influential woman and was later absorbed into the underground CCP. Somehow, she was named by a traitor of the CCP and arrested by the KMT's military spy agency. The underground CCP asked this prominent KMT figure to lobby on her behalf, and she was finally released on bail. After the communist takeover, she was assigned to a position in the RCCK in southern China. Apparently, this former KMT official never forgot his old love and he often found excuses to travel south to visit her. The UFWD knew of their relationship, and not only left them alone, but even facilitated their secret meetings, providing transportation. This prominent official was very grateful and never questioned the UFWD's directives, thereby becoming a leftist in the RCCK. As for lower-level non-CCP figures, if they were involved in any affairs that came to the attention of the UFWD, the affairs would became bargaining chips for the UFWD. Such transgressions could be considered large or small—if large, one would be labeled corrupt; if small, one would be considered romantic. This flexibility was fully utilized by the UFWD as a means of controlling its targets. Below are some examples.

1

A prominent figure in the business sector was one of the richest industrialists in the municipality, with capital assets estimated at 6 million RMB (equal to several hundred million RMB today) when Public-Private Partnership was implemented. He had studied in the United Kingdom when he was young. Tall and handsome, he had a wife and a concubine since before the communist takeover, the wife living in Nanjing and the concubine in Shanghai. He spent almost every weekend in Shanghai, either flying there or driving, returning on Monday. Although already over 60, he was still energetic, lustful, and not content with a wife and a concubine, so he had affairs from time to time. With government control very tight, there were no red-light districts, and it was also very dangerous for lovers to meet in a hotel room. To facilitate his "underground activities," this business magnate kept a bedroom on the third floor of a sales department building in the city center for his secret trysts. He often used his attendance at conferences as an excuse for not returning to his home in the suburb but staying overnight in the city, and in this way was able to entertain many women in this bedroom. Since the building was otherwise empty at night, his affairs went undetected for over two years.

During the Public Safety Bureau's campaign to crack down on rogues and vagabonds, an underground prostitution ring headed by a female sales assistant of a clothing store at the city center was uncovered after someone informed the authorities. Over twenty women between the ages of twenty and forty-five were implicated in this case. They were mostly married and all had jobs in stores or factories. They were generally very attractive and had banded together to make some money via illegal prostitution, targeting intellectuals and government and Party officials. Under the Public Safety Bureau's high-pressure interrogations, they exposed one another and were all arrested and jailed, becoming the largest underground prostitution ring ever uncovered in the municipality. During the interrogations, the prostitutes were all forced to describe their clients, and more than half mentioned an obese old man with fair skin who was energetic, fond of strange sexual positions, and very generous. They had all had sex with this man at the same address. Based on these confessions, the Public Safety Bureau quickly identified this high-profile business magnate and attached importance to this case by sending a deputy director general of the bureau to the UFWD to brief UWFD leaders to ask for instructions. The UFWD director general and his deputies held a special meeting and made two decisions: to immediately send two cadres to the Public Safety Bureau for further investigation, and to seek advice from municipal Party leaders based on developments in the case.

I, along with Mr. Wang, an old Party member in the Business Sector Division, was assigned to carry out this external investigation. It was arranged by the 4th Division of the municipal Public Safety Bureau that we would spend several days interrogating about ten female detainees individually. We were accompanied by a female officer in the Pretrial Division who used to conduct criminal investigations. Anyone could tell at a glance that she was an astute detective with a lot of experience. The interrogations were conducted in the interrogation room of the detention house, with the detective as the main interrogator and Mr. Wang and myself taking notes and asking questions.

This policewoman had a serious attitude and was extremely straightforward. After an opening statement about the policy of "leniency to those who confess," she asked each female detainee to clearly describe the details of her sexual encounters with the old business magnate. It turned out he was fond of oral sex, which at that very conservative time was considered perverse, so this detail was especially emphasized during the interrogations. The atmosphere in the interrogation room was quite stressful for us two males, who felt a strange shame while the two females were at ease, one asking questions and the other answering frankly.

During the breaks between interrogations, we analyzed the case with the policewoman and the director of the Pretrial Division. The director explained that, based on materials from reactionary cults uncovered in the past, some people used sexual intercourse to "borrow feminine force to strengthen male force" as in Taoist sexual practices, and hence he suspected that this businessman was possibly practicing a cult or seeking eternal life. This suspicion was endorsed by Mr. Wang, who had read about such practices in kung fu novels. The policewoman continued to solicit embarrassing details and repeatedly asked if drugs were used during the encounters.

When asked why they had agreed to have sex with this old man, most said it was for money. He paid 20 to 40 RMB each time, which was comparable to the monthly income of a third-level technician and could support a family of three people at the time. The food supply was very limited then and it was next to impossible to buy expensive groceries. A saying which circulated in factories at the time went: "Dropping your pants is better than working as a third-level technician." In reality, there were quite a few underground prostitutes in the community. However, since the CCP claimed prostitution had been eradicated in mainland China, organized prostitution rings as in this case were considered a serious crime. During the interrogations, we encountered a mother of three who explained through tears that it was all because her husband had been sent to a *laogai* camp and she herself earned too little. Her three kids were young and malnourished and she willingly sold her body in order to improve their condition. When she was arrested, the police officers at the local police station said as long as she truthfully confessed everything, she would be released soon. However, she had been in detention for over a year without being able to see her three kids. She begged for leniency so that she could take care of her children. Naturally, I felt pity for this young woman at the bottom of the social ladder and hoped she would be released and reunited with her family. Unfortunately, this prostitution ring was harshly sentenced, the ringleader getting fourteen years, and the lightest sentence being three years.

As for the business magnate, the CCP branch of the UFWD held deliberations and decided that there should be no punishment but that the businessman should meet with the UFWD director general, who would ask him to write a self-criticism. This was just to keep a handle on him: If he dared to commit any political mistakes, this shameful incident would be used against him. Of course, this was getting off light compared to the punishment of those miserable women.

When this business magnate met with the UFWD director general, he was scared to death because he didn't know how the CCP would punish him. He repeatedly said he deeply regretted his transgressions and would make a clean break with his past. He also promised in writing to follow the Party and give up his bourgeois lifestyle. Following this incident, the old man indeed always obeyed the UFWD's instructions and never dared to say or do anything beyond the Party line. He became very cautious and often voluntarily came to report his thoughts to UFWD cadres. He sometimes reported the business sector's current mentality to the secretaries general of the Two Organizations in order to win favor at the UFWD. Not only was his political status never unaffected by the scandal, but also he eventually rose all the way to vice chairmanship of the PCC. When he died in his eighties, the memorial service was very solemn, and he was called a close friend of the CCP and a prominent example of a democratic patriot.

2

A nationally renowned artist, whose paintings were praised by Mao Zedong, became a delegate to the National People's Congress. Although over sixty, he was very emotional and fond of the bottle. He would often drink until he became drunk. Many artists use alcohol to stimulate inspiration, as the poet Li Bai expressed it in verse: *"a barrel of wine leads to a thousand poems."* This artist often produced great paintings after drinking. Sometimes, after a meal and wine at an event organized by the PCC, the secretary general of the PCC would take out pre-prepared paper, paint, and painting brush, and ask him to paint anything at will. He would quickly produce a landscape or a painting of a bird and a flower, and the secretary-general would add it to his personal collection.

Because of the high value of his artistic creations, the UFWD gave this painter top-notch treatment politically and economically. He lived in a villa with a flower garden, and a dedicated car and a chauffeur were assigned to him. Many high-level officials of the CCP also liked to socialize with him in order to get his paintings and calligraphies. However, his fondness of drinking eventually got him into trouble. He had several children, and his wife was an elegant old lady who grew up in an upper-class family and was very intelligent and capable, expertly managing the household. However, perhaps due to a lack of caution on her part, a form of Trojan Horse entered the household. She was a maid hired from a nearby village to help with housework, who was in her twenties and already married. Although not an extraordinary beauty, she was nevertheless good-looking and voluptuous. In addition, she was very sweet and took very good care of the painter. Once, when his wife was out of town for a few days, he mistakenly entered the maid's bedroom when he was drunk. Having herself gone without sex for so long, the maid slept with him and they became lovers. They would have sex when his wife was away from home. However, the maid soon became pregnant, and her pregnancy was discovered by her husband when she returned home. She confessed who the father was and her husband came to the UFWD to complain and threatened to sue the painter. The UFWD was concerned that if the matter became public, not only would the painter's reputation be damaged, but two families would be adversely affected. After careful deliberation, the UFWD decided to downplay the problem and then trivialize it out of existence. The UFWD believed the maid's husband, who was a peasant, would agree to a monetary settlement. They dispatched two very experienced female cadres (a director and an officer) to negotiate with the husband. Eventually, the husband agreed to take a one-time child support payment of 40,000 RMB from the artist. This sum of money was astronomical at the time and could support a family of four for sixty years or fund the construction of a brick-and-tile dwelling with ten large rooms. The husband promised to keep the secret forever. Later, I learned that the unfaithful maid gave birth to a chubby baby boy, and the whole family led a life of plenty in their village.

When handling such a privacy-related case, the UFWD also went with the method of internal education and strongly criticized this famous artist, demanding that he produce a written self-criticism to keep in his files. Feeling guilty, the artist repeatedly denounced himself and promised to try his best to transform his thinking and never to drink too much again and suffer the consequences. However, he repeatedly dismissed his affair during conversations, claiming that it had only happened that one time. Later, the UFWD director general jokingly made fun of this artist: "This old womanizer only confessed to doing it one time. He thought it was like creating a painting so that one effort would produce an artwork. He is already over sixty, and it is shameless for him to say he could sire a son by doing it just once."

After writing a self-criticism that became part of his files, this respected artist lost his dignity and was always humble when meeting the UFWD director general, not daring to make eye contact. However, I didn't distain him and I still liked to chat with him and remind him to take good care of himself. Unfortunately, I soon heard the news that he had died of a heart attack. Later, during the Cultural Revolution, I heard that his children were persecuted. Hopefully, his illegitimate son in the village was safe and sound.

A nationally renowned business tycoon was worth over 100 million RMB in capital assets (probably equal to over 10 billion RMB nowadays) when the Public-Private Partnership was implemented. Other wealthy business people had already divided their assets while this titan in our province still remained the sole owner of his business, so he was probably the richest industrialist in the nation. Due to his high standing in the business sector, he was always among the presidium of the National People's Congress. Also, his son-in-law did business in Hong Kong, and when the CCP regime was short of foreign currencies during its early days, it borrowed foreign currencies several times through this son-in-law's firm.

This business tycoon grew his business through hard work and frugalness and was very conservative and law-abiding. However, his son became embroiled in a scandal. He had attended high school in Hong Kong and college in the US, and returned to China with a foreign diploma, although not from a top-notch school. He didn't learn much in the way of academics while overseas but developed a taste for the romantic lifestyle of the West. Since he was the sole heir of his father's assets in China, the UFWD arranged for him to serve nominally as a co-manager of a big textile plant in his hometown and a vice president of the municipal Federation of Industry and Commerce. However, he preferred the night life and mainly lived in a villa in Shanghai, taking the train to his hometown every once in a while to attend meetings. Since China was a closed society in the 1950s and 1960s, entertainment was pretty much limited to watching movies and strolling in the park. When this pampered son was bored, he would sometimes stroll down the streets to glance at young women, hoping to encounter a beauty.

On a fateful night, he did encounter a beautiful and well-dressed young woman on Nanjing Road. This lady was elegant and tall and walked like a foreign model, wearing a wool coat and a bright-colored wool scarf when most people wore indigo tunic suits. This young man was so attracted by her that he followed her almost to her home, where he started up a conversation by pretending to ask her for directions. This beautiful lady was happy to chat with a handsome young man wearing expensive clothes and a brand-name watch. The two soon fell in love as in a 1960s Chinese remake of an American love story. Although he learned that she was already married, he became so infatuated with her that he continued to meet with her secretly. Since a man and a woman had to show their marriage certificate in order to check into a hotel room at the time, they ended up renting a very small room as their love nest. After a while they attracted the attention of those old women on the street who were obsessed with class struggles. Someone reported to the community branch of the Public Safety Bureau that a suspicious lady had shown up, who was luxuriously dressed with an imported watch and jewels and was accompanied by a handsome young man, similar to underground CCP members in the old era. The Public Safety Bureau soon began investigating them as a case of "enemy situation," only to find out that he was the son of a business tycoon. This immediately became a political issue because, unlike today, having a mistress was considered a crime at the time. Shanghai UFWD immediately notified Jiangsu Province UFWD of this case and together they discussed how to proceed. Their decision was to employ internal criticism and education and keep the matter classified to avoid negative political consequences.

The UFWD leadership informed the business tycoon of his son's misdeeds in Shanghai. He was very upset and immediately recalled his son to Nanjing. The UFWD of his hometown counseled the young man, explaining that the lady was from the enemy class and intended to corrupt him. He was forced to sever his relationship with her under coercion and threat.

However, this pampered son had already reached thirty, and it was time to think of marriage arrangements. Therefore, it was decided that the UFWD and the Women's Association of his hometown should work together to find a beautiful bride. The search soon settled on a nurse in the outpatient department of the municipal hospital. This pretty girl was a typical beauty of southern China, had grown up in a humble family and had a pure and innocent heart. Following careful arrangements, the businessman's son pretended to be ill and went the hospital. The pair immediately hit it off and soon agreed to marry. Actually, there was a hilarious interlude in this arranged courtship. The beautiful girl had second thoughts when she learned that her fiancé was from a bourgeois family. If she married a member of the bourgeoisie, wouldn't it be a betrayal of her class? The UFWD worked together with the hospital's CCP branch to educate her on the Party's United Front policy, saying that this marriage was in the interests of the Party and would not impair her political progress. The wedding ceremony was on a grand scale and afterwards the newlyweds enjoyed a luxurious honeymoon in Hong Kong and Japan. Less than a year later, the girl gave birth to twin boys, and her parents-in-law were overjoyed. Every time the business tycoon met the director general of the UFWD, he always privately expressed his gratitude to the Party for educating his wayward son and guiding him down the right path.

At many holiday ceremonies, I saw this businessman and his wife along with their two lovely grandsons and their working-class daughter-in-law who wore expensive jewels just like a bourgeois lady. I wondered to myself, had the working class transformed the bourgeoisie, or vice versa?

However, behind the facade of this happy marriage, misfortune lurked. The beauty from Shanghai was destined to suffer greatly. When the "Four Cleanups Campaign" was carried out in the 1960s, she was sent to labor camp as a "bad element" and was later renounced severely during the Cultural Revolution. All her expensive possessions were confiscated. She lost her job and she was closely controlled by the community authority. It was clearly a case of "only seeing the smiles of the new love, without knowing the tears of the old love." Her life was ruined by this love affair that should never have happened. As the old saying holds, "beautiful girls have often an unfortunate life." In that era, a beautiful appearance was too often a source of misfortune.

Chapter 11: On-the-Spot Report of Hosting Li Zongren

In April 1966, I received a notice from the deputy director general of the municipal UFWD to attend an emergency meeting in the provincial UFWD's small meeting room for its leaders on the third floor of its office building. At the time, the provincial UFWD director general's office was next door to what had been the Presidential Office of the Presidential Palace in the KMT era. There were five people at the meeting: the provincial UFWD's director general, Mr. Gao, deputy director general Mr. Ye, office director Mr. Zhang, plus the confidential secretary and myself. The meeting was chaired by Director General Gao.

Mr. Gao first announced that Li Zongren, the former acting president of the KMT government who had returned to China from overseas, would be coming to Nanjing for a visit and sightseeing. Hosting Li Zongren would be an important political task that the provincial UFWD must complete to the best of its abilities as directed by the provincial CCP committee. A special host committee of five was hereby formed, with the director general and his deputy being team leader and assistant leader, respectively, and team members to include Director Zhang and myself.

Next, Mr. Gao read three documents. The first consisted of a speech by Li Weihan, head of the central UFWD, on the joint meeting of departmental leaders of the Party Central and leaders of the Ministry of Public Safety to discuss the hosting of Li Zongren. Li Weihan also conveyed Premier Zhou Enlai's directives concerning this task. This document was classified as top secret, and note-taking was forbidden. Based on my recollection, the document contained three parts: the political background of the return of Li Zongren, the Party Central's policy on Li's political arrangement, and the guidelines on external propaganda about Li's return.

In the first section, Li Weihan explained in detail the political background of Li Zongren's return to China, considering it a major success of the CCP's United Front work on the KMT after the establishment of the CCP regime. He elaborated on the process of United Front work on Li Zongren. A year before Li Zongren's return, his political delegate, Cheng Siyuan, came to the mainland from Hong

Kong and toured various places throughout China for over half a year, accompanied by a deputy head of the central UFWD. Cheng Siyuan received first-rate treatment everywhere he went and was shown newly completed engineering projects such as industrial plants in the Northeast and large hydraulic engineering projects, one of which was the Jiangdu Water Control Project in Jiangsu Province. Cheng Siyuan took photos of these achievements and showed them to Li Zongren in order to arouse Li's patriotic sentiment. He also conveyed CCP leaders' concerns about Li and their wish that Li should return to China. Because of Cheng's intense persuasion and Li's loneliness in the US (together with his knowledge that his wife had lung cancer and did not have long to live), Li finally decided to return to China. As a friendly political gesture, he began to reach out to Chinese-language media reporters in the US and praised the CCP's achievements in China. At this time, Chiang Kai-shek's KMT government in Taiwan followed Li's maneuvers closely and believed that the CCP's United Front work on Li, if successful, would have a great impact on Guangxi-Clique officials in Taiwan, and so the KMT must tightly monitored Li using its overseas spies.

However, the US government's attitude was completely different. High-level US officials, getting word of Li's plans to return to China, not only did nothing to hinder him, but secretly approved. Some members of Congress met with Li privately and expressed their hope that once he returned to China, he would try to persuade Mao and Zhou to end the military standoff with Taiwan so that mainland China and the US could open negotiations and even establish diplomatic relations. The FBI dispatched agents to enhance security around Li's residence. Since the PRC and the US had no diplomatic contacts at the time, these negotiations were top secret, and I believe this was the earliest signal of the change in the US government's China policy before Nixon's visit.

With the US and Taiwan having completely different attitudes toward Li Zongren's return to mainland China, Taiwan was afraid that the CCP would use Li's return to advance its United Front propaganda and dampen the morale of KMT officials (especially Guangxi-Clique military officers). For this reason, Chiang Kai-shek secretly ordered overseas spies to assassinate Li. In order to guarantee Li's safety *en route* to China, the CCP regime arranged for the PRC embassy in a foreign country to take Li from the airplane to the embassy directly to avoid KMT assassins, in a scene out of a spy movie.

Li Weihan said humorously that the Yankees should be thanked for Li Zongren's return, since without the United States' help, Li couldn't fly even if he sprouted wings! Li Weihan also pointed out that the US would never do a favor for nothing. They wanted to use Li Zongren to establish contact with the CCP and do a backstage deal. It was rumored that US officials hoped to persuade Chairman Mao and Premier Zhou to accept financial aid under the condition that China would agree not to attack Taiwan. To show political good will toward Li Zongren before he left the US, the Immigration Service granted reentry permits to Li and his wife and repeatedly indicated that if they couldn't adapt to living conditions in mainland China, they could return to the US any time, and would be welcomed back by the US government.

All of this was discovered by CCP spies in the US before Li arrived in China. Therefore, when Premier Zhou Enlai met with Li Zongren in Beijing for the first time, he stressed three points: First, all patriots were one family. Second, Li's return was a major historic contribution to the unification of China. In the future, Li could use his influence with KMT military and political officials in Taiwan to try to ease their concerns about what would happen after unification. Also, since Li had lived overseas for many years and had mainly heard one-sided stories about the Sino-US relationship, he should try to understand the situation better before getting involved. Third, China had made a lot of progress but our lifestyle was very different from that of other countries. For example, there were no night clubs or dance halls in mainland China, and some people missed such forms of entertainment after returning. The CCP's policy was that everyone who returned can freely leave again.

After meeting with Zhou Enlai, Li began to discipline his own words and actions as a political figure. In public places he never discussed the CCP's foreign policy. He only talked about his attachment to former colleagues and friends now living in Taiwan and about unification as the leading patriotic issue of the day.

To express his determination to remain in China, at a banquet that Peng Zhen hosted for Li and his wife on behalf of CCP leaders, Li gave his US green card and reentry permit to Peng Zhen and said that his return was "duty bound without looking back" and that he would "share both honors and disgraces with the motherland." However, his wife never surrendered her US green card and reentry permit till her death, probably because the couple still had children in the US.

Li Weihan's motivation in elaborating on the political background of Li Zongren's return was to ensure that those who were tasked with hosting Li would understand the importance of his return to the CCP's United Front work, and to emphasize the importance of security work.

Director General Gao then went on to announce the specific hosting plan for Li's trip to Jiangsu prepared by the provincial UFWD and approved by the provincial CCP office, and the report to the central UFWD. The report pointed out that the hosting of Li Zongren was a major political task and an implementation of the Party Central's important policy of United Front work toward KMT personnel. He claimed that Li's return was a great success of Mao's United Front thought. *Xinhua Daily* dispatched a reporter and a photographer to handle external reporting and publicity. The general agenda was to welcome Li's special train (since Li was treated as a national leader at vice-presidential level, his trips were equipped with a special train) at 3 pm on the first day and take him to his suite at Meiling Villa, which was formerly Chiang Kai-shek's suburban villa near the entrance road to the Sun Yat-sen Mausoleum and across the road from the State Guesthouse, where Mao Zedong and foreign heads of state stayed in. That night, provincial CCP secretary Jiang Weiqing would host a banquet for Li and his entourage in the Big Conference Hall of the provincial PCC, which was formerly the auditorium of the Presidential Palace of the KMT government. Attendees at the banquet would include all members of the provincial CCP secretariat, prominent figures of minor political parties, the governor, the lieutenant governor, the PCC chairperson and vice chairpersons, the People's Congress Standing Committee chairperson and vice chairpersons, UFWD leaders, the mayor of Nanjing, vice mayors, and prominent figures of the Nanjing municipal PCC. The whole second day would be spent touring the Sun Yat-sen Mausoleum and the tombs of Liao Zhongkai and Deng Yanda. The third day would include a tour of Mochou Lake, Xuanwu Lake, and the Yuhuatai Memorial Park of Revolutionary Martyrs. On the fourth day, attendees would tour local industries and the Fuzimiao District. The morning of the fifth day Li would meet with old friends in

Nanjing and that afternoon he would leave for Wuxi, where he would tour Lake Tai for the next three days.

Next, Director General Gao briefly described Li's entourage for this tour of the South (mainly Nanjing, Wuxi, Shanghai, and Hangzhou). According to the central UFWD, this would be Li's first tour after the death of his wife, Guo Dejie. Before Li departed, Premier Zhou asked him if he would like to take along some old friends to make the tour livelier. Li agreed and the central UFWD arranged for six people to accompany Li: former Guangxi-Clique figures Huang Shaohong, Huang Qixiang, the latter's wife, Liu Fei (member of CCP National Defense Committee and former KMT Defense Ministry Deputy Chief of Staff), Cheng Siyuan, and Guo Defeng (younger brother of Li's late wife, Guo Dejie, who lived in Switzerland and was visiting family in China). The two Huangs and Cheng were key members of the Guangxi Clique, whereas Liu Fei was an underground CCP member and spy in the KMT military, whose task was to do covert United Front work on Li Zongren while accompanying him on the tour. In addition, there was a representative of the central UFWD. Since Li's two previous tours included a deputy head of the central UFWD, this time Li Zongren explained that it would be unnecessary to assign a member of the central UFWD leadership, and that an officer would be sufficient. Therefore, the central UFWD dispatched Mr. Song, one of the secretaries of Li Weihan, to accompany Li Zongren. In addition, several attendants who were dedicated to serving Li Zongren as part of the vice-presidential treatment package would accompany him on this tour. Altogether, Li's party had twelve people.

As for Li Zongren's stipend and the standard of his boarding and meals on his tour of the South, Director General Gao and Vice Director General Ye explained that after Li's return to China, Zhou Enlai specifically asked Chairman Mao for directives about the political treatment of Li, and Mao indicated that "not following any standard" would be the best policy. He probably considered that Li's status in the KMT government was so high (he used to be acting president of the Republic of China) that the title of vice chairperson of the Standing Committee of the National People's Congress or vice chairperson of the national PCC would not be satisfactory to him. It was more appropriate to simple refer to him as a prominent patriot. Since Li didn't have any real political position, whereas salaries in mainland China were determined by administrative ranks, it was difficult to arrange for Li's salary. Zhou's solution was that he personally handed to Li Zongren a check for 200,000 RMB drawn from the State Council's special expense account after a private banquet, suggesting that Li open an account with the 200,000 RMB, and saying that if this turned out to be insufficient later, he could make a phone call any time for additional funds. Li was grateful and indicated that he had brought $50,000 along with him when he returned, and now that the government needed foreign currencies, he would like to donate it to the government for the development of the nation. Zhou answered that the government was not really short of money and suggested that Li create a foreign currency account in the People's Bank of China and withdraw the money at will. As for his residence in Beijing, a two-story villa in the west suburb was assigned to Li Zongren, where the late RCCK leader Li Jishen formerly lived. It had a garden and a garage, and was managed by the Administrative Bureau of the State Council.

Main Course of Hosting

At the time, low-level cadres like me didn't make a lot of money. At Administrative Rank 20, I earned about 70 RMB a month. Director Zhang at Rank 14 earned 120 RMB a month. We didn't have any decent clothes so, in order not to appear too shabby in front of distinguished guests, Director Zhang and I stopped by the Li Shunchang Western-Style Clothing Store to order suits. Director Zhang was formerly director of the Business Sector Division of the UFWD and was very familiar with this store's owner and his wife. We chose two pieces of woolen cloth, had ourselves measured, and placed emergency orders with next-day fitting and third-day pickup. I recall my suit cost over 80 RMB, more than my monthly salary. It was the first piece of clothing made of fine material I bought after I began working. When Director Zhang and I appeared in the new suits on Monday morning, he joked that we both looked like bridegrooms. I told him that I hadn't even worn woolen clothes at my wedding but only a khaki tunic.

At about 1 pm on the day of Li's arrival, Director Zhang and I received a notice that we would not go to Xiaguan Railroad Station to greet Li, but would go directly to Meiling Villa and wait there. At 2 pm, Director Zhang and I took a car to the State Guesthouse (where all the supporting staff would stay) across the street from Meiling Villa, checked into our room, left our suitcases there, and walked over to Meiling Villa. At its entrance, we saw ten or so plainclothes security officers strolling around apparently waiting for important guests. When we arrived at the doorkeeper's room, the chief of security immediately came to us, greeted Director Zhang, and shook hands with me, calling me by my name. Meanwhile, he directed us toward the main building. While walking, I asked Director Zhang why Chief Li immediately recognized me although I had never met him before. Director Zhang smiled and said this was what should be expected from professionally trained security cadres. They had previously seen our photos and hence could recognize us at a glance. As we were talking, we entered the reception room on the first floor of Meiling Villa, where Mr. Song, deputy chief in charge of interior security, explained the arrangement of rooms. This three-story villa was a fusion of Chinese and Western styles. There was a small meeting room and three guestrooms on the first floor. On the second floor was a large auditorium, where Mrs. Chiang Kai-shek had held Sunday services, and a large bedroom with a lot of sunlight which had been Mr. and Mrs. Chiang Kai-shek's bedroom and would now be used by Li Zongren. On the third floor were three bedrooms with private bathrooms, where three important guests accompanying Li would stay. This building looked like a western-style villa from below, but its large roof had Chinese-style blue glazed tiles. This fusion of styles created the impression of a man in a Western suit wearing a Chinese-style melon hat. It was probably an attempt to stay consistent with the blue glazed tiles of the Sun Yat-sen Mausoleum.

After taking a quick tour of all the floors and having a short rest, we heard the sirens of police cars and a long motorcade entered the compound. Mr. Li Zongren was in the second car, a Soviet-made ZIM sedan that was dedicated to carrying guests of head-of-state level and was the only car with bullet-proof glass in the province. The third and fourth cars were reserved for the director general and the deputy director general of provincial UFWD. The next cars carried Li's entourage, followed by a car carrying Li's security secretary and nurse, a reporter's car carrying *Xinhua Daily*'s journalists, and finally a rear guard car carrying several security officers. Such a long motorcade was uncommon in Nanjing, and wherever it went, police officers were needed to control the traffic.

After Li Zongren and his entourage came out of the cars, Director General Gao introduced them to Director Zhang and me in a small meeting room of Meiling Villa. General Gao described us as liaison officers specially assigned by the UFWD for their visit to Nanjing, and if they had any requests, they should feel free to reach out to either of us. Li and his high-level companions shook hands with us and then went to their bedrooms to rest before that evening's welcoming banquet in the auditorium of the former Presidential Palace.

Choosing this location instead of Nanjing Hotel, where banquets for most foreign visitors and political figures were held, had a special implication. As acting president of the Republic of China during the last stage of the Chinese Civil War, Li was the last head of state of the KMT regime on the mainland, and the Presidential Palace had become the office compound of the provincial PCC and UFWD. Having a banquet for the last supreme ruler of the KMT regime in the office building that he departed from seventeen years ago recalled the verse of the last emperor of the Southern Tang Dynasty: "*Those carved balustrades, those marble terraces, they should still be there; only the rosy cheeks have faded.*" Life is full of ups and downs and cannot be predicted! As the former owner of this residence and now the new owner's guest, Mr. Li must have felt a great deal of emotion.

This banquet was carefully arranged by the provincial Communication Division. Long octagonal lanterns were put up around the auditorium and fresh flowers covered the rostrum. The kitchen beside the West Garden Café was remodeled and enlarged to meet the demands of a large banquet. This event was attended by members of the provincial CCP committee, the government, the People's Congress, and the PCC, along with all the leading figures of the minor political parties. There were twelve tables and over 140 attendees. Several master chefs from top restaurants in the province were in the kitchen, including the head chef of the halal restaurant Ma Xiang Xing, where Li often held banquets for Guangxi-Clique figures when he was the Republic of China's vice president in Nanjing, and a master chef from the Hunan restaurant Qu Yuan, who was known for the entrée "Three Essence Chicken." The banquet was extremely sumptuous, demonstrating the grandeur of a large province.

The banquet was hosted by Jiang Weiqing, first secretary of the provincial CCP committee, and began with his welcoming address.

After that, Li Zongren read the address of gratitude drafted by Cheng Siyuan. This speech had a half-colloquial and half-archaic style to demonstrate Li's special historical and cultural background. For example, it contained such passages as: *"Revisiting old haunts and seeing the people living in peace and working happily in a flourishing city, different from the scene over a decade ago, as different as sky and earth, I couldn't help but sigh with great emotion."* A toast was drunk with Maotai liquor, and everyone appeared to be enjoying themselves.

Only Li's entourage, provincial-level officials, and directors general of the municipal UFWD were invited to the banquet. However, to accommodate Li's attendants from Beijing, two tables were served in the small banquet hall of the West Garden Café with the same courses as the main banquet. Besides Li's secretaries and attendants, there was a deputy director general of the UFWD, a director of the office of the provincial CCP committee, Director Zhang, and myself. Afterwards, Director Zhang said his meal was the best he had ever had in his life.

The second day's itinerary was to visit the Sun Yat-sen Mausoleum and the vicinity, including the tomb of Deng Yanda. The whole tour was accompanied by the director general and the deputy director general, two journalists, secretaries, Director Zhang, and myself. When paying homage at the Sun Yat-sen Mausoleum, Mr. Li scolded Chiang Kai-shek, accusing him of deceiving Sun Yat-sen and of executing Ouyang Ge, who was put in an important position by Sun Yat-sen and later served as commander of the navy. At Deng Yanda's tomb, Li strongly scolded Chiang for having Deng killed. Clearly, Li had broken off from Chiang long ago. I accompanied Li during the day and worked overtime at night to transcribe his exact words in briefings, which were sent to the central UFWD as express documents and published in a top-secret internal briefing titled *Zero Newsletter*. This newsletter's scope of distribution was limited to no more than forty people, including members of the Central Politburo and secretaries of the Central Secretariat. It was also one of Mao's favorite internal briefings. Afterwards, I realized that the reason the central UFWD asked us to report every word and action to the Party Central was to entertain Mao during his leisure time. Obviously, in Mao's eyes Li Zongren's return was like a treasure seized from the enemy in a war. In this way Mao could show to the world what a hero he was. Now the whole country supported him and the Guangxi Clique had become his special guest. As for Li Zongren, he continuously scolded Chiang and sang the praises of the CCP. The petty officers of the UFWD couldn't take a rest and had to work until 2 am or 3 am at night, because the drafts of briefings had to be reviewed and modified by Director Zhang, submitted to the typist, and sent to Beijing no later than the afternoon of the next day.

The third day's itinerary was to visit Mochou Lake, Xuanwu Lake, and the Yuhuatai Memorial Park of Revolutionary Martyrs. Along the way, Li talked about urban development and praised former Mayor Shi of Nanjing, who followed French urban development to plan two arterial roads, Sun Yat-sen Road South and Sun Yat-sen Road North, and planted London planetrees along both sides of the roads, which had since fully grown and provided a great deal of shade. When visiting Yuhuatai, Li avoided talking about the KMT's killing of CCP members there and spoke instead about the Nanjing Massacre by the Japanese army. He told how the Japanese army broke into Nanjing through Zhonghua Gate near Yuhuatai, and how the KMT army bravely defended Nanjing and suffered great casualties. When he recalled WWII, he repeatedly observed that the Chinese army was ill-equipped but its bravery and sacrifices were unparalleled. If we had been as well-equipped as the Japanese, we would never have allowed them to occupy over half of China. Listening to Li, I felt the awe-inspiring presence of a famous general who commanded several hundred thousand Chinese troops at Taierzhuang. At Yuhuatai, we also encountered a group of students from the high school for returned overseas Chinese, most of whom had returned from Indonesia. They didn't know that this skinny old man who walked with a cane and climbed steps slowly was previously an influential figure on the battlefields of WWII. Noticing these students' uniforms, Li learned they were returned immigrants and affectionately waved to them, saying that he was also a returned immigrant and that all Chinese wished to return to their homeland.

On the morning of the fourth day, we toured the Nanjing Radio Factory and the Cloud Brocade Institute. Both were model enterprises of Nanjing's industrial development, which Li paid special attention to. When the factory manager told him their Panda Brand radio had been exported to Southeast Asia, Li observed that China's industries had started late and we had to work hard to catch up with Europe and America.

In the afternoon, we went to see the market at Fuzimiao. The Security Section's original plan was to have Li and his entourage remain in their cars, which would be driven slowly around the market. Over three hundred plainclothes security officers were dispatched along the path through Fuzimiao, with over a third inside the market itself. Since the plan was a car tour, the market was not cleared, and ordinary people were allowed to stroll the market. When the motorcade arrived in front of Dacheng Hall, Mr. Li on a whim suggested getting out of the car and walking a bit. The chief of the Security Section obtained permission to let Li walk about 200 yards. After the motorcade stopped, the chief of security was busy instructing plainclothes security officers to pay attention. However, after Li exited his car, because of his appearance and the news of his activities in Nanjing over the previous three days, he was immediately recognized by the public. The news spread quickly, and Li had only walked twenty steps or so when he was surrounded by a large crowd. To show his gratitude, Li frequently waved his hand, which attracted even more attention. After a couple minutes, over two hundred people had gathered around. While directing plainclothes officers to form a protective circle, the chief of security tried to prevent the crowd from closing in on Li, but the people were too excited, so Mr. Ye, deputy director general of the provincial UFWD, requested Li be brought out immediately. The chief of security had to act quickly. He signaled the ZIM car to drive up, and when the car doors were opened, Li was immediately thrust into the back seat. With over ten plainclothes officers clearing the road, the car slowly drove out of Fuzimiao and returned to Meiling Villa. Mr. Ye kept apologizing to Li, saying that they hadn't made proper arrangements and had chosen a bad location to stop the car, where there were too many people in the crowd. Li accepted the apology and told Mr. Ye not to worry.

That night, Peng Chong, secretary of the municipal CCP committee, held a farewell banquet for Li and his companions, who would leave for Wuxi the next afternoon. The banquet took place in the Nanjing Hotel and was smaller than the welcoming banquet with just six tables.

The morning of the fifth day was reserved for Li to meet with relatives and old friends in Nanjing. When asked in advance whom he wanted to see, Li only had mentioned one person: Shi Fangbai, vice president of the provincial CPWDP, who was nearly 80. We learned that when Shi served as director general of the Finance Department of Anhui Province under Governor Li Pinxian during WWII, he allocated substantial funds to Li Zongren's Fifth Theater of Operations to support the Guangxi-Clique troops' supplies. When Li learned that Shi was still alive, he was eager to meet with him. As a straightforward man loyal to friends who didn't like the fawning of officialdom, Shi was not favored by the CCP after the communist takeover. He only had the title of PCC member and provincial CPWDP vice president. In the UFWD's internal political ranking, he was always considered a rightist under internal control. Li and Shi were excited to see each other, talked for about two hours, and then had lunch together. Afterwards, the UFWD sent a so-called leftist cadre of the CPWDP to Mr. Shi's home, who asked Shi what he and Li Zongren had talked about. Shi said they had just reminisced about their work in Anhui and Li had asked about some of his former subordinates, many of whom had already passed away. Some of them had been executed during the Campaign to Suppress Counter-revolutionaries, but Shi was sensible and didn't mention this to Li.

A ridiculous incident that was connected to this meeting occurred later during the Cultural Revolution. In 1967, I was visited by several teams of special investigators and questioned about Li Zongren's visit to Nanjing. There were rumors that Li visited a prison where he saw a KMT spy, who used a secret code to tell Li which spies were still alive; Li's wife, Guo Dejie, immediately used a radio transmitter in one of her teeth to send the intelligence to the KMT. Because of such ridiculous rumors, many former Guangxi-Clique members and former KMT figures that Li Zongren had visited became suspects, and special investigation teams were formed to arbitrarily investigate and apprehend spies. Every time I received such so-called "special investigation team" members wearing red armbands, I refuted the rumors and guaranteed that Li only met with one person in Nanjing, Shi Fangbai, and asked them to stop such arbitrary investigations and spare the innocent.

After his lunch with Shi, Li left Nanjing on a special train for heads of state, which had bedrooms, bathrooms, a small meeting room, and a dining room. Mao Zedong also traveled in such specially equipped trains. Actually, a train between Nanjing and Wuxi only took a little over two hours, but for Li's security and status a special train had to be assigned.

At Wuxi, Li was greeted by the mayor, vice mayor, and PCC chairperson. His long motorcade, led by police vehicles, went directly to the Liyuan Hotel. This hotel was on the shore of Inner Lake Tai and was formerly a private residence with a small western-style building and a large garden. Later, two small two-story villas were constructed beside the lake. One was called Distinguished Guest House No. 1 and was surrounded by great views of the lake in three directions. When foreign heads of state visited Wuxi, they always stayed here. Li was to stay in this villa. His entourage would stay in House No. 2, which had smaller bedrooms and faced the lake in two directions. Between these two villas and the original building, there was another two-story building with eight guestrooms, where Deputy Director General Ye, Director Zhang, the two journalists from *Xinhua Daily*, and myself were to stay.

That evening, the Wuxi municipal CCP committee and municipal government held a banquet in the big living room of the villa where Li stayed. There were six tables and over sixty people. Since I came from Nanjing, the Communication Division arranged for me to sit on the main table for distinguished guests, and specially arranged for me to sit beside Mr. Cheng Siyuan, because he and I not only shared the same surname but also differed by only one character in our given names. At the beginning of the banquet, the director of the Communication Division introduced all the distinguished guests. When Cheng Siyuan heard my name, Cheng Ganyuan, he grabbed the name card from in front of me and said: "What a coincidence! I met someone from the same clan today." We soon realized we were not from the same clan, but the surname Cheng originated from one source in Henan Province and we joked that five hundred years ago we had been family. Mr. Cheng Siyuan joked that my given name was better than his because "Gan" is to take action, which leads to knowledge. I countered that his name was better because "Si" is to have sophisticated thoughts and have politics in command. "As the ancients said, actions succeed after thorough thoughts and fail if blindly following others." We both laughed.

This banquet was one of the most luxurious I had ever seen. The dishes consisted completely of fish and other seafood. The most impressive dish to me was the "braised Lake Tai carp." When a carp over a foot long was served on the table, its mouth was still opening and closing as if alive, which scared some people off. It was crispy on the outside and delicate inside, truly delicious. Another impressive dish was Lake Tai ice-fish and tofu. The tofu was shaped like buns and was put into a hot broth with live ice-fish. The ice-fish bore into the tofu balls to escape the heat. The broth would then be heated until boiling, and minced green onion and seasonings would be added before serving. According to written records, Wuxi's fish culture goes back to ancient times. The assassination of King Liao by Zhuan Zhu at a banquet using a miniature sword hidden inside a baked fish took place here in the 6th century BC. The story of using a fish dish to help kill a tyrant has long been a warning to despotic officials who crave power, lead a corrupt life, and oppress the common people.

The whole next day was devoted to a yacht tour of Lake Tai. The boat belonged to the provincial Public Safety Department and was dedicated to hosting heads of state and CCP leaders. It was said that Mao Zedong had toured the Lake in it many times. We stopped for a tour of Sanshan Island, where we had Wuxi refreshments for lunch, including small wonton soup, soup-filled buns, Wuxi braised pork with gluten, and Wuxi sweet and sour ribs.

During the lake tour, I had casual conversations with Mr. Li Zongren and Mr. Guo Defeng. I asked Mr. Li if he had toured the US and learned he didn't travel much while in the US. I then told Mr. Li that I supposed it was a good feeling to now be relieved of official duties. "Like a bird in the sky, you can now go anywhere you like." Mr. Li agreed. When I asked Mr. Guo about his life in Switzerland, he said he ran a small hotel, where the first floor was a restaurant and the upper floors were guestrooms. There were many such family hotels in Switzerland. The staff was all college graduates who knew several languages, including French, German, and English so that guests would feel at home. Mr. Guo remarked that China had vast resources for tourism; for example, some locations around Lake Tai were no worse than Switzerland, and it was a pity that they had not been developed for tourism.

The next day we toured the Mei Garden, which was the private residential compound of the famous Chinese business titans Rong Jingzong and Rong Desheng brothers. It had classical Suzhou-style landscaping with running waterways and was famous for its spectacular plum blossoms. There were also many precious flowering plants and bonsai. When we were strolling along a winding trail surrounded by porous stones, Mr. Huang Shaohong suddenly sighed and said there was no path out. Liu Fei immediately responded with the verse "*Suddenly one encounters the shade of a willow, bright flowers and a lovely village.*" At night, I immediately wrote down the conversation between Huang Shaohong and Liu Fei in the form of a briefing for the central UFWD's *Zero Newsletter*. I attempted to contrast the political views of the two men. Since I had a talent for detecting political trends, my briefings were well received by Party Central leaders, and I was frequently praised by UFWD leadership.

Another detail worth recalling is that when Li Zongren toured Mei Garden, in order to preempt the embarrassment of a crowd as in Fuzimiao, the provincial Public Safety Department decided to close the garden to the public, ostensibly to do restoration work. However, in order that Li Zongren not feel separated from the people, many police officers were disguised as tourists, including some pairs that were disguised as couples and some with young children. This kind of deception for the sake of security or propaganda was commonly used by the CCP regime. Director Zhang and I didn't know this in advance but quickly figured out the tourists were police officers in disguise. He whispered to me that once Chairman Mao stayed at the No. 3 Hotel in the eastern suburb and the Public Safety Department dispatched a director disguised as a waiter. This director was tall and well-built. Chairman Mao figured out right away that he was not really a waiter, and asked: "Old comrade, when did you start working for the Party?" The director was very embarrassed and murmured: "Quite a few years! Quite a few years!" Afterwards, the Public Safety Department reprimanded the director of the Security Division: "Why did you dispatch such a senior cadre to serve meals? You made us lose face!"

In the afternoon on the third day, the director of the municipal Communications Division, hoping to win favor with Li Zongren, took Li and his companions to Xiaoqi Mountain to tour Mao's small villa. Xiaoqi Mountain was actually a small island on the northeast side of Lake Tai connected to the lakeshore via a small concrete bridge. There were many trees around this small island that made buildings on the island invisible from the lakeshore. Our motorcade entered the island via the bridge and passed by several garages and single-story buildings. After we got out of the cars and walked south, we saw a

European-style two-story building. This exquisite building was formerly a private villa of Wuxi business titan Rong Desheng. There were only three rooms on the second floor, the southernmost of which had a semicircular window ledge and large windows affording panoramic views of water and sky and giving the impression that the whole building was surrounded by the lake. When it was windy, one could see majestic waves on the lake. This was really a heaven on earth. I felt that Chairman Mao owned the most beautiful scenery in all China.

What amazed me even more was that Mao not only enjoyed the scenery here but also was accompanied by an exceptional beauty. When we arrived at this small villa, we were greeted by a tall lady of unrivalled beauty with the face of a movie star and the figure of a super model. She looked to be in her twenties. Although she was only dressed in a simple white smock like a doctor, her elegance and grace were immediately felt. She seemed to be on good terms with the director of the Communications Division and greeted him familiarly. The director told us this building had two attendants, one male and one female, dedicated to serving Chairman Mao. They lived here all year round, always ready for Mao's visit. It was said that this was Mao's second favorite touring destination after West Lake in Hangzhou. His longest stay here had been a month, while his usual stays were two weeks or shorter. Seeing this beauty, I couldn't help wondering if Mao had an affair with her. Any man in the presence of such a beauty must be aroused.

Li Zongren spent four days and three nights at Lake Tai. Because of his tight agenda, the original plans to visit Suzhou were cancelled. Instead, a documentary about classical Suzhou gardens was shown in the small meeting room of Li's villa.

At 10 am on the fourth day, Li and his entourage left for Shanghai in his special train. The director general and deputy director general of the UFWD, Director Zhang and I all went to the train station to see them off. Before boarding, Mr. Cheng Siyuan spoke to me, saying: "Brother Ganyuan, you've worked hard these past few days. We are really grateful and look forward to seeing you again."

Chapter 12: On-the-Spot Report of Hosting Former POW's

Mao considered the defeat of the KMT regime during the Chinese Civil War (1946-1949) as one of his two greatest achievements (the other being the Cultural Revolution). Mao implemented the policy of combining punishment, control, and mind transformation of the over three hundred prisoners of war that were captured in this conflict, plus over twenty officials of Manchukuo who were captured by the Soviet army at the end of WWII and transferred to the CCP. These POW's received special pardon after the ten-year anniversary of the founding of the PRC, and became targets of United Front work after their release. This was considered an important success of United Front work. In the spring of 1963, the UFWD of Jiangsu Province and the provincial and municipal PCC's arranged to host the so-called Tour Group of Culture and History Experts (internally referred to as the Tour Group of Specially Pardoned POW's). The following is a detailed description of the POW's background and the tour group's course.

Two months before the celebration of the ten-year anniversary of the founding of the PRC, Mao Zedong, as chairman of the CCP Central Committee, wrote a letter to PRC president Liu Shaoqi to suggest releasing a batch of POW's. At the time, over three hundred POW's were imprisoned in Fushun POW Detention House in Northeast China. On September 17 of that year, the Standing Committee of the National People's Congress discussed Mao's suggestion and passed the Resolution on Special Pardon of Rehabilitated Criminals. On the same day, Liu Shaoqi issued a Decree of Special Pardon by the President of the PRC. On December 4, the first batch of thirty-three POW's, including Du Yuming and Aisin Gioro Puyi, were released. From then on, the Supreme People's Court released POW's in five batches as stipulated in the National People's Congress resolution. By the beginning of the Cultural Revolution in 1966, 296 POW's had been released and the remainder had died in prison.

The Tour Group of Specially Pardoned POW's that the National PCC organized in the spring of 1963 were mostly settled in Beijing and assigned to positions such as commissioner of the PCC's

Committee of Cultural and Historical Materials and member of the Culture and History Institute of Beijing Municipality. They were high-ranking POW's, including the emperor and ministers of Manchukuo and major generals and higher officers of the KMT military.

The Committee of Studies of the national PCC had over forty members, including fourteen specially pardoned POW's and their family members. It was led by Chen Cisheng, a member of the national PCC's standing committee. Since the visitors were all high-level figures of the KMT and top Manchukuo officials, the provincial and municipal UFWD's did extensive preparation work. The provincial UFWD held a special meeting of all the provincial and municipal UFWD officers in the Political Parties Divisions who would participate in the hosting, together with cadres of the PCC secretariat and the provincial Communication Division, to divide up the work. The PCC secretariat owned the itinerary and would send cadres in advance to the chosen tour locations to prepare the greeting ceremony, the tour itself, and the meals. The Communications Division arranged for boarding, transportation, and security. The Political Parties Divisions of the provincial and municipal UFWD's were responsible for briefings and news reports.

Additionally, a working team was formed, which mainly consisted of RCCK members who did preparation work for the provincial PCC. In charge was Liao Yunze, deputy secretary general of the PCC, who was a lieutenant general of the KMT's left-behind troops, defected to the CCP, and was also a student of the first graduating class of Huangpu Military Academy. The hosting team had ten members, including the following former KMT generals: Hang Hongzhi, lieutenant general and dean of the KMT regime's Central Military Academy; Xiao Pingbo, major general and division commander in the Southwest who defected to the CCP; Wang Yanqing, Commander of Nanjing Garrison who defected to the CCP; plus two recently released POW's, Chen Changjie, lieutenant general and commander of Tianjin Garrison, and Qiu Xingxiang, major general and commander of Luoyang Garrison.

After this meeting, the UFWD asked some leftists in the RCCK such as Qiu Xingxiang and Lai Ti'an to pay attention to the trends among members of the tour group, i.e., to report in a timely fashion their words and actions to the UFWD to facilitate the writing of briefings. The tour was scheduled after the CCP's Beidaihe Conference in 1962, when the political winds changed. The Intellectual Work Conference's policy of relaxing class confrontation by adjusting relationships and treating intellectuals well was replaced by "never forgetting class struggles" and understanding new trends in class struggles. After the relaxation of rural area policies in 1961, some areas implemented a policy of "three individuals and one fixing." "Three individuals" referred to the policy of allowing peasants and small businesses to take individual responsibility for their own profit or loss, of permitting self-management by individuals, and distributing small plots of land for individual use. "One fixing" meant allowing fixed output quotas on a household basis instead of higher levies on higher output. Because of these relaxed economic policies, the rural economy—which had been bankrupt by the Great Leap Forward, the strictly egalitarian distribution of food and consumables in communes, and free allocation of labor and materials without compensation—began to recover to some extent, and food supplies increased. However, Mao Zedong looked into "new trends in class struggles" and imagined he saw a conspiracy to negate the Three Red Flags (the General Line for Socialist Construction, the Great Leap Forward, and the people's communes). Therefore, the Tenth Plenary Session of the Eighth Central Committee of the CCP suddenly issued a political warning that class struggles should never be forgotten. To cater to Mao's political preference, the central Propaganda Department demanded that education about "Three Ism's" (patriotism, socialism, and internationalism) be carried out among all people across the nation. The PCC was stimulated by the political wind and proposed in its Committee of Studies that "Three Ism's" education should be carried out among all sectors and drafted and implemented plans at all levels of the PCC.

The POW tour group as organized by the national PCC was also responsible for implementing this policy, and arrangement of the tours had to reflect the directives concerning the visitors' "Three Ism's" education. On the one hand, the service should ensure that the visitors eat and sleep well; on the other hand, the transformation of minds should be promoted through "Three Ism's" education during the tours.

The specific activities were as follows:

At about 4 pm on May 15, the tour group's train arrived at Xiaguan Railroad Station, where they were greeted by secretary generals of provincial and municipal PCC's. Then they all checked into Nanjing Hotel, which was usually used by the Communications Division to host foreign guests. At about 6 pm, they were treated to a banquet in a festive setting in the auditorium of the former Presidential Palace. This was the first time I saw Emperor Puyi and some high-level officials of the KMT regime. They all wore teal-colored wool tunic suits, which were probably tailored for them after they were pardoned and arrived in Beijing, in order to make them presentable when they met with Premier Zhou Enlai. Most of the family members wore western-style clothing, while the wife of Du Yuming stood out by wearing a long Chinese dress, jewels and makeup. My first impression of Puyi was that he looked like an elementary school teacher. With his lean physique, his spectacles, and his humble smile, no one would think that he was the last emperor of China. The most active attendee of the banquet was Shen Zui, who kept making toasts with provincial and municipal leaders and cracking jokes with Puyi. He told Puyi that this palace was formerly the site of the Mansion of the Viceroy of Liangjiang, and this auditorium was also regal at that time, but it could never be compared to Puyi's Forbidden City. Puyi smiled and said there were different levels: the Viceroy of Liangjiang was the emperor's commissioner and was only at the level of minister when in the capital; if the auditorium was built too large, it would offend the emperor and be considered treasonous. Shen Zui also said to Du Yuming that this auditorium was where Chiang Kai-shek gave his weekly talks in memory of Sun Yat-sen, and that Du probably heard some of his talks here. Du said it had been like a child monk chanting the scripture from memory and without his heart in it. The speaker spoke and the listeners listened.

On the morning of the first day of the tour, the group visited the Nanjing Radio Factory, which was a symbol of the industrial development of this municipality and had already been visited by Chairman Mao. There were many banners there with the slogan "Go all out, aim high, and achieve greater, faster, better and more economical results in building socialism." The chief engineer of this factory, who had worked as an engineer in the KMT's military telecommunication factory, gave a presentation about the factory's production. He explained that the factory was going to produce black and white TV sets, and the visitors seemed very excited about this. Actually, color TV's were already being mass-produced abroad, but everything started from scratch in this factory and they were impressed by the progress that had been made. In the afternoon, the group visited the Nanjing Automobile Factory, which was largely staffed by the auto repair corps of the KMT army. Among the hosts were an engineer who had formerly been the deputy regimental commander of the KMT's automobile corps in Xuzhou, was captured there, joined the PLA to do auto repair, and later became a director-level engineer at the Nanjing Automobile Factory. When he saw Du Yuming, he saluted Du respectfully and said: "Welcome, Commander Du." Du was embarrassed and rushed to shake hands with him, saying: "We parted over ten years ago and I never anticipated seeing you again in Nanjing. Now that you are a member of the working class, I should learn from you. I am ashamed." At the discussion forum, KMT general Wang Yaowu said: "Our army's US-made automobiles couldn't run faster than the PLA's two legs. Success and failure are really determined by the people's sentiment." It was an emotional moment.

On the morning of the second day of the tour, the group visited the Sun Yat-sen Mausoleum. When they were paying homage, I noticed that several KMT generals were using their handkerchiefs to wipe away their tears. Afterwards, we rested at the tea parlor in front of the mausoleum, and provincial RCCK figure Mr. Liao commented that Dr. Sun wanted to ally with the Russians and the communists, but Chiang insisted on anti-communism, and we all followed Chiang, so we were bad students of Dr. Sun. Everyone nodded.

After lunch at the Linggu Temple Café, the group toured Xuanwu Lake. For the sake of security, the park stopped selling tickets to the public in the afternoon except for group tickets to some schools, enterprises, and institutions. Many members of the tour group had been to Xuanwu Lake before and recalled their previous visits.

On the same day, the tour moved to Fuzimiao. To show that the former sex industry at Fuzimiao had been eradicated during the socialist transformation, the district government and sub-district office invited a former dancer in the sex industry who was now a textile worker to give a talk. This lady was very eloquent and vividly described the misery of prostitutes at Fuzimiao in the old era and how they were transformed after the communist takeover. The visitors liked her talk and felt enlightened. However, one of the visitors commented with sentiment: "They prostituted themselves in the old era, and we risked our own lives in the military, so she and we should quote the verse '*Abandoned by the world, you and I are both big losers. Why should we have acquainted ourselves with each other before we meet one another?*'" Another member of the tour group felt uneasy at his negative tone and refuted: "We should say that we are all transformed new persons and are brought together today through destiny." The group roared with laughter.

The tour of Yuhuatai Memorial Park of Revolutionary Martyrs on the third day was the highlight of the entire trip. This was a deliberately arranged "class struggle education." First, the group viewed the exhibits of martyrs' deeds at the Martyrs Museum, where they not only listened to the curator humbly and respectfully but also took meticulous notes. At the exhibit about Liu Shaoqi's former wife, He Baozhen, who was executed by firing squad at Yuhuatai, some wiped away tears and some commented that President Liu had been devoted to revolution, but despite the killing of his wife, he still issued the decree of special pardon for us, which indicated that the communists were broad-minded.

Next, the tour went to Jiangdong Gate to visit the commemorative site of the Nanjing Massacre, where a memorial was being planned. The site was not open to the public yet, and the tour group only viewed the mass grave. These generals who fought the Japanese invaders on the battlefields of WWII had never forgiven the Japanese army for its cruelty.

In the afternoon, a special symposium was held for the tour group to express opinions about that morning's tour. When discussing the Memorial Park of Martyrs, Song Xilian confessed that the biggest regret of his life was carrying out Chiang Kai-shek's order to execute former CCP leader Qu Qiubai in 1936. He described Qu Qiubai's calm manner before his execution, and stood up to bow to Qu's spirit three times. When discussing WWII, the former generals described their troops' desperate fights on the frontlines against the Japanese. When Chen Changjie recalled how he led his troops to into hand-to-hand combat with the Japanese and eliminated a whole regiment of the enemy, he was radiant with excitement as if he were once again a powerful general commanding thousands of troops. During the break, a few RCCK cadres accompanying the tour felt that the direction of the symposium was wrong in that it appeared that WWII in China had been fought by the KMT military while the CCP army wandered around with nothing to do. They decided to redirect the meeting's topic. After the break, a so-called leftist of the RCCK gave a talk in which he attacked the KMT military for being responsible for the Nanjing Massacre because the KMT's defense of Nanjing utterly collapsed and the commander Tang Shengzhi fled. Some tour group members angrily wanted to hold Tang Shengzhi liable. Others came to Tang's defense, saying Tang had become a member of the national PCC's standing committee because of his contributions to the CCP during the Chinese Civil War, so let bygones be bygones. These discussions became vivid material for my briefings. I wrote a briefing that night and sent it to the central UFWD the next day.

On the fourth day the group visited the October Commune in Qixia District, which Chairman Mao had visited previously. This commune and its cheating of visitors by displaying goods borrowed from the Export Corporation were described in Chapter 9.

On the fifth and last day of the group's visit to Nanjing, they were allowed to engage in their own activities in the morning and could meet with relatives and friends. At lunchtime, the hotel's café provided meals and waived the requirement of food rationing coupons. Tour group members could show their room card and bring their guests to the café for lunch. Some had dozens of guests, and the café staff was kept busy until after 2 pm.

At 5 pm, the visitors left for Shanghai on a train. They would spend a few days there before moving on to visit Hangzhou. UFWD cadres and secretary generals of provincial and municipal PCCs went to the railroad station to see them off. Mr. Shen Zui shook hands repeatedly with Director Liang of the UFWD Political Party Division and with myself, and expressed his gratitude and his wish to see us again.

Chapter 13: "Rightist Transformation Office"

Historical Review of the Anti-Rightist Campaign

The Anti-Rightist Campaign of the 1950s in Mainland China was a historical tragedy of large-scale political persecution of intellectuals, and was the beginning of Mao's complete betrayal of the democratic ideals that he had once advocated before seizing supreme power. From that point on, Mao restored imperial despotism and became the cruelest and most cold-blooded ruler in Chinese history. Since Qin Shi Huang, many emperors had persecuted intellectuals for their writings or political opinions, but none of these persecutions could compare to the Anti-Rightist Campaign of the 1950s and the Cultural Revolution of the 1970s and 1980s in terms of scale and number of people affected. Nearly 60 years have passed, and most victims of the Anti-Rightist Campaign have died. Few of those rightists in their thirties at the time are still alive today, and those younger than thirty were a small portion of all rightists and are in their eighties now. Most people born after the 1950s in Mainland China know little about this episode of history because of the CCP's selective teaching of history. When they see scenes of this campaign in literature or movies, they can hardly imagine such events truly took place. What's more, current cadres in the UFWD have little knowledge of the "Rightist Transformation Office" that the UFWD formerly operated. As a witness to history, I feel obliged to recall this episode of history as a form of eulogy for those who were persecuted to death during the Anti-Rightist Campaign and those victims who have died after surviving the extended persecutions.

As the political organization with the largest membership in Chinese history, the CCP, for historical and cultural reasons, not only was unable to stop Mao Zedong's plot to entice dissidents to voices their opinions and then crack down on them, but collectively participated in this campaign of persecution. As a consequence, it must be held liable politically. All CCP members with conscience should reflect on this organization's political crimes. However, very regretfully, the CCP official stance to this day is still that the Anti-Rightist Campaign was necessary and that it "only erred in exaggerating the scope." Their justification is that there were indeed rightists who threatened the Party at the time. The guilty verdicts of several rightists have still not been overturned as of now, including those of Zhang Bojun and Luo Longji, president and vice-president, respectively, of the CDL who served as government ministers, and Lin Xiling of People's University. Keeping several "correctly labeled" rightists was meant to vindicate Deng Xiaoping, who said the Anti-Rightist Campaign was correct in its intent but was taken too far. Ironically, Deng actually served as the Party Central's Director of the Anti-Rightist and Rectification Office!

To restore the true history, I would like to elaborate on my own experience during the Anti-Rightist Campaign before describing the "Rightist Transformation Office" that the UFWD set up in 1961.

In 1957, I was studying law at Fudan University in Shanghai as a cadre-transfer student from the military. I was 20 and very ardent and ambitious. As a Korean War veteran and someone who had served as a local branch secretary of the Communist Youth League, I had recently become a preparatory member of the CCP in September 1956. In 1957, the school was immersed in an atmosphere of intense study, adopting the slogan of "Marching to Science." The first thing we would do after dinner was to rush to the library with our satchels of books to occupy a good seat. Sometimes a roommate would be sent to occupy several seats, because there were not many seats in the library and latecomers would have to go to the classrooms to study. This indicates how enthusiastic we were as students at the time. Most students studied sciences and wanted to become the next Madame Curie, Hua Luogeng, Michurin or Pavlov, while those studying law hoped to follow in the footsteps of Vyshinsky (a Soviet jurist). While we were hard at work, a political movement suddenly loomed on the horizon.

In March 1957, Mao declared in the Central Working Meeting on Propaganda that the Party Central planned to start an intraparty rectification campaign that year. On April 27, the CCP Central Committee officially issued its Directive about Rectification Campaign, which was published in *People's Daily* on May 1. This directive stated that, since many comrades tended to solve problems via simple administrative orders, those who didn't have a firm stance could easily pick up traces of the old era, develop a sense of privilege, and even employ means of persecuting the masses. Therefore, it was necessary to carry out a deep and widespread rectification campaign throughout the party against bureaucracy, factions, and subjectivism. The directive also stipulated that the correct handling of conflicts among the people should be the main theme of rectification. It emphasized that this rectification campaign should be serious while sympathetic, appropriately involving criticism and self-criticism, using the method of individual heart-to-heart talks or small discussions and not those of big meetings or public denunciations. Proceedings should follow the principle of "everyone with opinions should talk; everyone who talks should fully express opinions; do not blame the man who speaks but heed what you hear; correct mistakes if you have them and guard against them if you have not."

To facilitate this rectification campaign, Mao Zedong invited leaders of all minor political parties to a symposium on Tian'anmen Rostrum and asked them to help the CCP in this campaign. On May 4 the Party Central issued a "Directive about Inviting Non-Party Figures to Help with Rectification," which emphasized that non-Party figures' participation in the Party's rectification forums and teams should be in the form of raising complaints and criticisms to the Party and not expressing self-criticism. The Party Center indicated that it sincerely welcomed criticisms and complaints from non-Party figures no matter how sharp they were, and that over 90% of the criticisms appeared to be honest and justified, which would prove very helpful in correcting mistakes. The Party Center also warned that some Party members had thoughts against the people and didn't respect non-Party figures. Common, although not prevailing, this situation must be corrected immediately.

Many naïve intellectuals believed Mao's solemn vow to invite non-Party figures to help with the Party's rectification and loyally put forward suggestions to the Party. In Shanghai, municipal CCP committee secretary Ke Qingshi also held many symposiums for non-CCP figures. Among the attendees were some nationally renowned professors of Fudan University, including Sun Dayu of the Foreign Languages Department, Yang Zhaolong of the Law Department (formerly Prosecutor General of the KMT government who ordered the release of over 400 underground CCP members before the communist takeover of Nanjing, and could be said to be of meritorious service to the CCP), Jia Tuofu of the Chinese Language and Literature Department, and Tan Jiazhen of the Biology

Department. A symposium of the art and culture sector in Shanghai was attended by Mao Zedong in person.

Less than two months later, the political atmosphere had changed significantly. In June, Mao Zedong's essay titled "Things are Changing" was distributed to CCP members, in which he argued that "rightists have been the most determined and the most arrogant in minor political parties and higher education institutions lately" and that "we should let them behave savagely for longer and let them reach a climax." Under Mao's directive, the CCP Central Committee issued an internal directive that the provocative remarks of those who had anti-communist sentiments should be published without modifications in newspapers, and that the CCP's refutation should be withheld temporarily so that the reactionary nature of rightist remarks could be revealed.

In early July, **People' Daily** published two editorials, **Wen Wei Po**'s "Bourgeois Orientation Should Be Denounced" and "The Working Class is Speaking Out." A rapid campaign of class struggle began to escalate throughout China. By 1958, over 550,000 people were labeled rightists.

At Fudan University, big-character posters suddenly covered the campus in 1957, followed by large-scale debates. The university branch of the Communist Youth League asked those students who were CCP and CYL members to actively participate in debate meetings organized by each department. A student of the Physics Department named Ma Mingmin put up a big-character poster to criticize the university CCP committee's leadership of the school as laymen leading experts and to advocate autonomous governing of universities by faculty. Among students, small discussions emerged spontaneously, mainly revolving around dissent from the Leaning-to-One-Side policy toward the Soviet Union, socialism vs. nationalistic Chauvinism, and Tito's speech in Pula, the full Chinese translation of which was published in **People's Daily**. The Law Department also discussed Yang Zhaolong's challenge: "Why don't cadres doing legal work understand legal education?" In the Law Department, Yang Ming of Class No. 2 and Xing Shifang of Class No. 3, both cadre-transfer students from the military, bravely expressed some personal opinions about Tito's speech, claiming that Tito broke the dogmatism of Stalinism, that socialism should guarantee the people's right to democratic participation in politics, and that it was wrong to lean to one side and blindly follow the Soviet Union.

The CCP branch of the department continued to hold discussion meetings of Party members among students and urged members to be on their guard, to distinguish between right from wrong, and to have the courage to fight misguided views. Student Party members were also told that this was the moment to test their character and determination and that they should continue to hold meetings and embrace new trends. Soon *Wen Wei Po* published an editorial criticizing Wang Zhong, who served as Fudan University's dean and was a CCP committee member and chairperson of the Journalism Department, maintaining that Wang Zhong's bourgeois views of journalism should be challenged. This led to an upsurge of debates throughout the university. Some students and admirers of Wang Zhong put up big-character posters to refute the editorial, saying that journalists should not serve as the Party's mouthpiece and that reporting should follow the basic rules of journalism. After that, several large debates were held in the Journalism and Physics departments, where I witnessed the impressive performance of several outstanding students. Ma Mingmin, a short, slender girl with spectacles, spoke calmly in front of several hundred people and maintained that science had nothing to do with class, and the development of science was not up to the will of the CCP. I was deeply moved and shaken by this girl's martyr-like resolve. Because of her grasp of truth, everyone who attempted to refute her in the debates was defeated. On the fourth day, the Party Organization orchestrated some students to denounce her by disclosing that she originated from a questionable background and harbored class hatred toward the CCP. They interrupted her speeches many times to overwhelm her with their numbers, turning the debates into a denunciation. Ma Mingmin became the first Fudan University student to be labeled a rightist. She was later dismissed from the university and sent to labor camp. When her case was redressed in the 1980s, she already looked old and her hair had turned grey. Similarly, a high school classmate of mine, who was an outstanding student, was labeled a rightist at Tsinghua University.

Perhaps most disturbing was the fate of my Fudan classmate Xing Shifang. He was from Shandong province and his parents had died when he was young. He joined the communist revolution when he was 14 or 15 and participated in the Battle of Jinan as a scout, where he was rewarded for meritorious services. Later, he worked at the Public Safety Bureau of Jinan and enrolled in Fudan as a cadre-transfer student in 1955. Since he was strongly in agreement with Tito's speech in Pula, a classmate who was a member of the university CCP committee reported him to the department. (This individual was later promoted to the position of student CCP committee secretary because of his firm stance during the Anti-Rightist Campaign.) A special debate meeting was held for Xing Shifang. Since he considered himself a revolutionary cadre without any disloyalty to the Party and didn't believe that his opinions about Tito's speech affected his political position, he failed to denounce himself and was labeled an extreme rightist because of his insistence on his reactionary stand. As fate would have it, one day he was in a bookstore reading a book and forgot to pay for it before leaving. The store clerk believed he intended to steal the book and refused to accept his explanation that he had just forgotten to pay. When he showed his student ID, the bookstore seized it and turned him over to the Security Division of the university, which discovered that he was a rightist. The university decided to impose aggravated punishment. He was dismissed from school and escorted back to his hometown in Shandong to do agricultural labor under supervision, where he eventually went insane. When his case was redressed in the early 1980s, he came back to Fudan alone. As many school officials who had witnessed his misfortune in the 1950s were still there, the school gave him 500 RMB and asked him to return to his hometown. No one knew his whereabouts afterwards. All his classmates participated in renouncing him, and since we respected him initially as a veteran cadre and didn't renounce him harshly enough, we were criticized by department leadership for not taking a firm stance. We felt his punishment was excessive, but since he had a political label already, no one dared to champion his cause. Recently, I made some inquiries into his whereabouts in order to give him some financial assistance, but I was unable to locate him.

Where are you, Xing Shifang? Your classmates in the Law Department all failed you, and I didn't say any comforting words to you back then because I was worried about my own future. Over fifty years have passed, and we must all face the judgment of history. We can only silently repent and pray for you. If only someone had shown you some compassion and love, you might still be alive and in good health today.

The official number of rightists nationwide was over 550,000, but the real number was actually higher because some people were labeled rightists in 1958 after confessing their opposition to the Party during the rectification and confession movement. This grouping of rightists were mainly elite intellectuals. Their conditions became unbearable and many committed suicide. For example, my distant uncle Cheng Shifan, who had been the vice-chair of Anhui province PCC and a delegate to the National People's Congress, hanged himself in 1961 in his hometown after suffering for his rightist views. Some were imprisoned in labor camps for many years and survived in extremely poor condition.

In August 1959, Mao Zedong wrote a letter to Liu Shaoqi to suggest removing the rightist label from those who had been transformed before the ten-year anniversary of the founding of the PRC. On September 16, the CCP Central Committee issued a directive to remove the rightist labels from about 20% of all rightists, and promised to eventually do the same for the others. About 45,000 rightists (less than 10% of the total) had their labels removed in the first batch. In September 1961, the central UFWD, Organization Department, and Propaganda Department jointly held the first "National Working Conference on the Transformation of Rightists" and proposed to remove the labels from 30% of rightists in 1961. They followed the Party leadership's directive to form a "Leading Team for Rightist Transformation Work" consisting of cadres from the UFWD, Organization Department, Propaganda Department, Political and Legal Commission, and the Cultural and Educational Commission. The Office of Rightist Transformation Work was set up under the UFWD to run its daily affairs. About 100,000 rightists had their labels removed that year. After the second National Working Conference on the Transformation of Rightists in 1962, the central UFWD proposed to remove the labels from 70% to 80% of rightists, but soon after that the Party took a turn to the left at its Beidaihe Conference and the Tenth Plenary Session of the Eighth Central Committee of the CCP. Under the slogan "class struggles should never be forgotten," no one dared to talk any longer about removing rightist labels.

What I Heard and Saw at the "Rightist Transformation Office" in Nanjing

Around the time I started working at the Nanjing municipal CCP committee UFWD, its Office of Rightist Transformation Work (commonly known as the "Rightist Transformation Office") was established. At the time, it consisted of only two cadres. One of them, Mr. Hou, was a former regiment-level military officer who began working for the CCP during WWII and was assigned to the Rightist Transformation Office after retiring from the military. He wasn't especially educated but was very cordial and honest. Although he had the title of Director at deputy division level, everyone called him "Old Hou." The other cadre, Mr. Liu, was an officer transferred from the Organization Department who handled day-to-day work. He used to be a shop assistant and was promoted several times for his activism in denouncing the bourgeoisie during the Three-anti and Five-anti Campaigns and the nationalization of private capital. Although he was not well educated either, he displayed an arrogance of power because he was dispatched by the Organization Department to manage other cadres. He often spoke with a non-respectful tone about his superior, Old Hou, and behaved as the representative of the Rightist Transformation Office on all occasions. To show that there was a clear dividing line between him and the rightists, he often gazed at visiting rightists with contempt and defied them to make eye contact with him.

At the time, rightists of this municipality who lost their jobs numbered over two thousand. They were concentrated in four agricultural camps: Qixiashan, Jiangpu, Fangshan, and Lishui. These were all former labor camps to detain *laogai* inmates and had been converted to reeducation camps. Some rightists had their labels removed after 1960, but their former employers refused to rehire them and they arranged to remain in the camps as "staying workers." They were mostly former teachers and staff members of elementary and middle schools, and a few were former cadres, college and vocational school students, and technical employees of factories and mines. They received only slightly higher stipends than *laogai* inmates. Usually, those with rightist labels only received about 26 RMB a month, and those who had had their labels removed and become workers of the camps received third-level technician compensation at about 36 RMB a month. Their management was handled by the

139

Public Safety agencies, and they had to act collectively. The difference between those with and without rightist labels was that those without the labels could have a weekend day to rest and could leave the camp with permission from managing cadres. Those with labels were allowed to take a day off to rest, but could only stay in the camp unless under special circumstances. This was similar to the treatment of *laogai* inmates.

As a result of the great famine at the time, grain and grocery supplies were very limited and the rightists in camps were all malnourished. Their clothing was ragged because of hard labor in the field, and in general their conditions were miserable. The purpose in creating the Rightist Transformation Office was to review the implementation of the policy on the transformation of rightists; for this purpose, UFWD leaders accompanied by Rightist Transformation Office cadres sometimes visited the camps to inspect their work. Before each visit, the camps would conduct cleanups, issue every rightist new clothes, and put up banners everywhere reading, "Welcoming Leaders' Inspection" and "Building the Camp into a Big School of Maoism." To make a positive impression on UFWD leaders, the camp would also add some meat to the diet of rightists. A few role models were chosen to take part in a symposium, where they would report their takeaways from the transformation and receive the encouragement of the leaders. The camp management would treat the visitors to an excellent lunch and sometimes give them some melons and fruits to distribute to UFWD staff. I was responsible for writing up such activities into briefings in order for upper-level UFWDs and the municipal CCP secretariat to learn about the achievements of rightist transformation work.

However, what we encountered on a daily basis was quite different. Often one or two former rightists who stayed in the camps as workers would come to the UFWD to petition. They would wait in the doorkeeper's room for a cadre of the Rightist Transformation Office to meet them. They wore ragged clothes, had uneven haircuts, and looked famished. Some who were in their thirties appeared to be over fifty. During the winter, they still wore thin clothes and sat curled up like beggars. If they were lucky, Old Hou would receive them and lead them inside to the small meeting room, where they could sit down while talking and pour some hot water from the thermos to drink. If they were received by Officer Liu, they were less fortunate. Liu would not begin with asking why they had come to petition but would assault them with stern words, such as, "Why don't you work hard in the camp to transform yourself?" He usually didn't allow them to enter the compound and only talked to them briefly in the doorkeeper's room before telling them to leave. Obviously, these people would not have walked 20 kilometers or more to the UFWD if they had not had compelling reasons. Their complaints usually concerned illegal actions on the part of camp cadres, such as punishing them with very high workloads, not giving them their stipends, not allowing them to see the doctor when they were sick, or not allowing them to marry.

I recall that a man and a woman came to the UFWD in the early half of 1963 to petition for approval of their marriage. The man used to be a cadre-transfer student at a university and the woman had been an elementary school teacher. They were both labeled rightists and went to the same labor camp, where they cared for each other and fell in love. Later, they both stayed in the camp as workers. They decided to get married and asked camp management for approval. At that time, it was necessary to have a letter of approval from your work unit in order to register for marriage at the government's Civil Affairs Section. However, their request was ridiculed by camp management, who criticized the couple for not working hard to transform themselves, but instead developing a romantic relationship. In these cadres' eyes, rightists were class enemies who didn't have the right to become involved romantically. Therefore, camp management was sure to come up with excuses for denying their request. Several times this pair of lovers had to walk long distances to the UFWD to petition for what was their basic right. I sympathized with the young couple. If Officer Liu was out and I saw them, I would lead them to the small meeting room and serve them hot water. Officer Liu disapproved of my kindness and said they were dirty and would stain the sofa in the small meeting room. I greatly resented Officer Liu's attitude and wondered why this cadre from the working class only recognized people's clothes and not their dignity. Finally, their true love moved the deputy director general of the UFWD, who said: "Cadres of the camp are really unreasonable. They are both over twenty-five, and no provisions in the marriage law prohibited them from marriage. Rightists are free to fall in love like anyone else. The camp is not a monastery!" Because of the deputy director general's insistence and her warnings that if camp management didn't produce a letter of approval within one week they would be considered in violation of the Party's policies and reported to the municipal CCP committee for punishment, camp management finally produced the letter. A month later, this couple came to the UFWD wearing neat tunic suits and gave a pound of fruit-flavored candies to UFWD cadres to show their gratitude. When Officer Liu distributed the candies, he remarked with ridicule: "Eat the rightists' wedding sweets!" When eating the candies from this couple, I felt a strange sour taste in my heart. Nevertheless, I sincerely wished them a lifetime of love together.

Chapter 14: Control and Management of Religion

1. The Essence of the CCP's Religion Policy

The CCP's treatment of religion is based on the so-called Marxist theory of religion. From the standpoint of dialectical materialism and historical materialism, Marxism took three positions on religion: First, religion originated from human delusions regarding the natural world and social phenomena. Religion is irrational and opposed to science, so all religions in the world are illegitimate. Second, Marx and Engels viewed religion as a tool used by the exploiting class and labeled it "class suppression" so as to incite anti-religion sentiment among the proletariat. Marx famously referred to religion as "the opium of the people." Third, the political party of the working class should have a policy toward religion of long-term struggle, gradual restriction and eventual elimination. Marx and Engels both recognized that religion as an ideology could not be eliminated using the same method as was used to eliminate the bourgeoisie. They believed that it would require a long historical process to eradicate religion.

In its very essence, Marxism is opposed to freedom of worship. Marx attempted to use atheism to establish a Marxist religion among the people with the "heaven of communism" as the enticement. This cult has led mankind into self-destruction, while Marx has been portrayed as the universal savior.

Nowhere in the world, including in religious fundamentalist countries, do political parties fear and hate religion as much as the CCP. In this, the CCP is like a conman who has defrauded the people of huge sums of money and is constantly worried about facing trial in a court of justice once his frauds have been exposed.

The CCP's so-called freedom of religion is the most hypocritical policy in the world. Its officially published "Basic Views and Policies about Religion during the Socialist Era of Our Country," which is still in effect today, publicly cites Marx's theory of religion as mentioned above. How can a party that aims to eliminate religion offer the people true freedom of religion?

After the CCP regime was established in 1949, religion was increasingly severely attacked in political movements. According to statistics, members of the Roman Catholic Church, Protestant churches, Taoism, and other religions numbered between five and six million in China in the early 1950s. During the Campaign to Suppress Counterrevolutionaries, from 1950 to 1952, many members of the clergy were imprisoned or executed as "reactionaries who are against the people's government and collude with imperialist forces." Among them, the Roman Catholic Church's Legion of Mary and the Taoist offshoot Yiguandao were considered counterrevolutionary organizations. Not only were their clergy executed, imprisoned, or thrown into labor camps, but their members were all required to register as members of counterrevolutionary organizations. During the Great Leap Forward and the "Socialism Education" movement, many churches and temples were demolished, many practitioners were forced to terminate religious activities, and many monks and nuns were forcibly secularized. During the Cultural Revolution, religion was devastated, and many innocent practitioners were denounced or killed. Mao's wife, Jiang Qing, even shamelessly claimed that "Religion in China has become history." When the Cultural Revolution came to an end in 1976, only 700,000 to 800,000 religious practitioners remained in China, and the majority of these worshipped underground.

After the Reform and Opening-up policy was implemented, religion in China revived rapidly. The CCP's official count of religious practitioners in China today is over 100 million, and the actual number may exceed 300 million. Surely it is God's plan to purify the soul of the Chinese people. After suffering under demonic forces, they crave the light of life.

2. Party and Government Institutions for United Front Work on Religion

The CCP has realized that religion belongs to the domain of ideology and can't be banned and eliminated using brute force, so it has adopted an approach of restriction and control plus monitoring, education, and propaganda to gradually restrict religion and create fissures among high-level religious figures. The core of Mao's religion policy is still among the central UFWD's published guidelines: promote atheism; crack down on any crimes that take

144

advantage of religion; insist on the principle of independence (i.e., no ties with the Vatican or other foreign churches); and cultivate patriotism (which actually meant loyalty to the Party) among clergy. The key strategy is to restrict religious freedom, sever international connections, and closely control the clergy. As for such concepts as freedom of religion and protection of legal rights, they are for outsiders who don't understand the CCP.

No other political group in the world has felt the need to commit so many resources to fight religion as the CCP. Presently, the central UFWD has a Bureau of Ethnicity and Religion (also known as Bureau No. 2) for United Front work on ethnic minorities and religion. At the local level, provincial UFWD's usually have a Division of Ethnicity and Religion led by a deputy director general, and municipal or county-level UFWD's have either a Division or Section of Ethnicity and Religion or assign a deputy head to do this work. Since it is inappropriate for the UFWD as a Party organ to directly manage ethnic and religious affairs, the government system also has an Ethnic Affairs Commission and a Religious Affairs Administration at the national level and an Ethic and Religious Affairs Bureau, Division, or Section at provincial, municipal, and county levels.

When I entered the Nanjing municipal CCP Committee UFWD, China was in dire financial straits after the Great Leap Forward, and the Party Central issued a directive to simplify institutional structures and reduce staffing. The Nanjing municipal UFWD had only one deputy director general dedicated to ethnic and religious affairs. He belonged to the Hui ethnic group (a Sinicized Muslim people in China), but as a veteran underground CCP member had rejected most Muslim traditions and even ate pork to demonstrate the atheism of a communist. However, his mother and his wife were pious Muslims, and he was a filial son, so he strictly followed Muslim traditions at home and didn't allow anything containing pork or lard to come through the door.

At the time, municipal governments in China combined their ethnic affairs, religious affairs, and overseas Chinese affairs functions into one institution called the Division of Ethnic, Religious, and Overseas Chinese Affairs, following the Party Central's directive concerning institutional sequestration. This division in the Nanjing municipal government had a director, a deputy director, and four sections (Section of Secretariat and one for each of the three functions). The whole division had a total of twelve cadres, fewer than three per section. Its office building was separated from the UFWD compound by a wall and people could go from one institution to the other using a door.

The director of this division was an old cadre who joined the CCP in the early years of WWII and did intelligence work for the underground CCP for many years. Originating from the landlord class, he had always been given a hard time during the CCP's rectification campaigns for his family background. During the Cultural Revolution, he was even labeled an "alien element of the class" and suffered greatly. The reason for his harsh treatment was usually related to his ties to his parents, who were landlords. His first offense was that when he went back to his hometown as a cadre of the military administrative council after the communist takeover, he took along a gun and fired two shots off a bridge near the village to show off his status as a revolutionary cadre. This was interpreted as a show of support for his landlord parents and a disregard for his communist status. His other offense was that after land reform was implemented in his hometown, his parents as former landlords lost everything and couldn't survive, so they went to the city to live with him. This was labeled "shielding a landlord." Later, around the time of the Great Leap Forward, he had to send his parents back to his hometown under pressure from the Party Organization, and his parents died there during the Cultural Revolution. While it is human nature to want to support one's parents, it was denounced by the CCP as insisting on a reactionary position and disloyalty to the Party. This CCP cadre who came from the wrong class was traumatized by repeated political movements and became extremely cautious and timid, always obeying his superiors without question. Each time a political movement took place, he would engage in another round of self-criticism, harshly criticizing himself for not having a clear stance on class and not being loyal to the Party. After each movement, he was always reinstated to his original position, where he served as an "old director" for over 20 years. Actually, he had a bachelor's degree and was very shrewd and energetic when doing intelligence work in the underground CCP, only to become a "second-class cadre" after the CCP seized power. Every time I saw him wearing inexpensive clothes and looking humble, I thought that the CCP's "class origin" criterion was really misguided, and that were he a KMT intelligence officer during WWII who retreated to Taiwan after the civil war, he would at least be made a general because of his standing as a war hero.

The deputy director of this division was an old cadre who came from the peasant class and joined the CCP in its rural base area during WWII. Since he was authentic "Old Eighth Route," his status was very different from that of the director. Although he was only a deputy director at two ranks lower than the director, every time there was a political campaign, he always became the head of the leadership team of the division and actively denounced the director. Such a strange relationship between superior and subordinate was not uncommon in the CCP. Among the CCP's cadres, there were a number of "leftist" loyalists who were the most active supporters and the most loyal executors of Mao's extreme-leftist policies. Mao's strategy was to use internal conflicts to control cadres, believing that the Party would never lose its vigor as long as internal conflicts existed.

3. Using Religious Organizations to Control Religion

Since it was considered inconvenient for the CCP to manage and monitor religious activities directly, this was done via religious organizations. After the CCP established its regime in mainland China in 1949, in order to sever the ties between Chinese religious organizations and international ones, the CCP engineered the "Three-Self Patriotic Movement" of Chinese Christians. This movement was nominally initiated by over forty pastors, led by Rev. Wu Yaozong, and called for ending imperialist control and achieving the "three selves" of self-governance, self-support, and self-propagation. The National Committee of the Three-Self Patriotic Movement of the Protestant Churches in China was established, together with the China Christian Council. Later, the Chinese Patriotic Catholic Association and the Bishops' Conference of the Catholic Church in China were founded in order to counter the dictates of the Pope. The national organizations of Buddhism, Taoism, and Islam were also founded, and today mainland China has seven officially sanctioned religious organizations. These appear to be independent non-governmental organizations but are actually external organs of the CCP's UFWD and the government's Religious Affairs Administration. The methods of control and management are as follows:

First, personnel salaries and expenditures are all allocated from state funds as part of administrative budgets. Their employees and full-time leaders are all part of the administrative institutional staff and receive compensation at half a rank lower than the administrative rank of the government religious affairs agencies they report to. Some high-profile religious figures who are PCC standing committee members or vice chairpersons are treated as belonging to bureau or sub-provincial levels. Therefore, strange terms such as "bureau-level bishop," "division-level pastor," and "section-level imam" have become common in China. Not only were their salaries paid by the state, but their regular expenditures were written by the UFWD into its general administrative budget. Non-recurring large-scale religious events like the commemoration of the ancient Monk Jianzhen's Mission to Japan had their budgets specially prepared by the UFWD and allocated as special United Front spending after approved, similar to the budget of the annual *lianghui*. During the three years of the great famine in the early 1960s when mainland China was in a severe financial crisis and many people were starving, the PCC budgeted over 30,000 RMB (over 3 million RMB today) on banquets for superiors and prominent figures, such as the banquet after each biweekly symposium held by provincial and municipal CCP secretaries and UFWD directors general.

When I worked at the UFWD, its central policy regarding prominent religious figures was to organize them to conduct political studies and transform their minds via the PCC's Committee of Studies. Besides PCC members, religious figures who were People's Congress delegates and religious organization leaders were also included in the Committee of Studies and were required to attend four or five half-day sessions every week. Those religious organization cadres who were not included in PCC's Committee of Studies were organized into a Joint Study Team and came to the PCC to listen to reports and participate in small-group discussions. Their words and actions during the studies were all summarized into written reports based on meeting minutes provided by leftists in the religious sector. The reports were sent to the UFWD, where briefings about trends in class struggles among the religious sector were published irregularly. The CCP never loosened its control of religious figures and continued to instruct them in atheist Marxism ideology.

Second, some CCP members disguised as members of the clergy are directly assigned to leadership positions in religious organizations. For example, one of the main leaders of the National Committee of the Three-Self Patriotic Movement of the Protestant Churches, Li Chuwen, and the nationally renowned Buddhist Zhao Puchu, were both CCP members who joined the underground CCP during WWII. Li Chuwen studied in the US as a leading member of the Christian Youth Society, and returned to mainland China after the communist takeover. Zhao Puchu became a leader of the National Buddhist Society. Their CCP memberships were kept secret, and they reported directly to a vice head of the central UFWD. Their special status was used to mislead some religious practitioners into believing that their praises of the CCP were God's will. Using religion as a political tool was a trick that the CCP deployed before it seized power. Nowadays, if any religious person still believes the CCP's alleged "separation of church and politics," he must be possessed by an evil spirit.

The CCP regime also directly assigns CCP cadres to places of worship, where they serve in the management or as clergy to directly control religious activities and monitor practitioners. Therefore, there are fake Buddhist monks, fake Christian pastors, and fake Taoist priests in mainland China who detect every action of religious practitioners and frequently report to the UFWD, sometimes with grave consequences. For example, the municipal Public Safety Bureau's First Division (in charge of political security) assigned a phony monk, who joined the CCP military during the Chinese Civil War as a scout, to the biggest Buddhist temple in Nanjing, where he compiled detailed reports. Once, a regiment-level military officer and his wife went on a pilgrimage to a temple to pray for a son and make a donation. The fake monk sensed the high social status of this worshipper and approached him to talk about Buddha's teachings, thereby winning his trust. This military officer gave his name and address to the monk. Soon, the UFWD figured out his identity and wrote a special briefing to warn against the infiltration of religious superstitions into the military. Soon afterwards, this unlucky officer was discharged from the military and sent back to his hometown.

Interestingly, perhaps because of karma per Buddha's teachings, this phony monk was later beaten up by Red Guards during the Cultural Revolution, who demanded that he confess to engaging in superstitious activities. To protect his life, he revealed his real identity as a secret police agent. The Red Guards didn't believe him in the beginning and came to the UFWD for verification. Since he had already revealed himself, the UFWD had no choice but to confirm his identity. Since then, he could no longer stay in the temple. After the Cultural Revolution, he was reassigned to the Cultural Heritage Management Commission and was given the political label of "a CCP member who failed to withstand the test of hardship."

4. Using Religious Leaders' Privacy to Control Them

The CCP's tactics toward religious leaders are twofold: attacking and exploiting. Prominent religious figures are bribed using political assignments and economic benefits. For example, shortly after the establishment of the CCP regime, several pro-CCP religious figures were assigned to become PCC members and People's Congress delegates. Those who were loyal to their religions and didn't play up to the CCP were suppressed in various political movements. For example, many clergy members were arrested during the Campaign to Suppress Counterrevolutionaries, and the Legion of Mary was banned. Many religious figures were arrested and jailed, such as Cardinal Ignatius Kung Pin-mei, who was sentenced to life in prison. Many were executed or died in labor camps.

Concerning those religious figures with a track record of misconduct, as long as they are loyal to the CCP they will be put to use. For example, when I worked in the Nanjing municipal UFWD, a priest of the local Catholic diocese was highly corrupt, having even cohabited with a nun for many years since long before the communist takeover and had children with her. The UFWD helped him to legalize this relationship as a registered marriage, but he soon seduced a younger nun, who also gave birth to a son. In order to take advantage of his influence, the UFWD always helped to settle his family conflicts and tacitly approved of this abnormal marriage of a priest and two nuns. After the priest died in the 1970s, to preempt any dispute between the two nuns, the UFWD arranged for two separate memorial services, one for each of the nuns.

Another example was a womanizer monk whose sexual relationships with many pilgrims were eventually brought to light. He should have been labeled a sexual predator and kicked out of the monastery, but because he was able to flatter the Religious Affairs Administration leadership and informed against some counterrevolutionaries hidden in the monastery during the Campaign to Suppress Counterrevolutionaries, he was thought to be of meritorious service to the Party, and the Religious Affairs Administration leadership did its best to absolve him from guilt and downplay his misconduct as a trivial issue. In the end, he not only received no punishment at all, but also became a PCC member and a leader of the local Buddhism Society.

The UFWD's treatment of these corrupt religious figures has a political logic. Just as a deputy director general in charge of religious affairs said, "The CCP is atheist and never cared about monastic discipline or celibacy. As long as a clergy member regards the CCP as the true god, we should not be bothered with trivial life affairs." As long as the CCP has information that can be used against these religious imposters, they can easily be manipulated by the Party.

Chapter 15: United Front Work with Overseas Chinese

The CCP regime's local-level governments all have an Overseas Chinese Affairs Division (commonly known as an Overseas Chinese Division) led by the Overseas Chinese Affairs Office of the State Council. In the Party hierarchy, each Overseas Chinese Division is managed by the UFWD. In municipalities with many relatives of overseas Chinese or many who have returned to China, the UFWD specifically has a division or office or a deputy head dedicated to overseas Chinese affairs.

Before the Cultural Revolution, following Mao's Class Struggle theory, the CCP viewed overseas Chinese as an exploitable force in external class struggles and made use of some pro-CCP overseas Chinese community leaders to create a pro-CCP atmosphere in diplomatic venues. At the same time, the CCP's overseas intelligence agencies, such as the Xinhua News Agency, tried their best to recruit pro-CCP figures among overseas Chinese organizations to collect intelligence. Southeast Asia had the largest number of overseas Chinese. According to the CCP, among the over 30 million Overseas Chinese, Southeast Asian countries were home to over 10 million. Since Hong Kong and Macao residents were also considered overseas Chinese at the time, the total number was even higher.

The CCP's overseas Chinese policy was always two-faced. Those living overseas were welcomed with smiles to win them over. Once they returned to China and became domestic residents, they were regarded as outsiders. From the class struggle point of view, they had lived for an extended time in a foreign country, had received an imperialist education, belonged to the bourgeoisie and were unable to adopt the communist worldview. According to the CCP's paranoid logic, former overseas Chinese who returned to China must be either losers unable to survive overseas or imperialist spies with hidden missions, because it was unimaginable that anyone who had led a comfortable life overseas would abandon his bourgeois world view and embrace the low standard of living in China. The political review files of some intellectuals who returned to China contained labels of "spy suspect" or "use under control." Such tarnished files would follow them, without their knowledge, all their lives.

After the CCP's large-scale internal review and examination of cadres in the mid-1950s, "overseas relationships" became a dreaded political label. No one with this label could enlist in the military, be promoted, or admitted to the CCP, or work in public safety or judicial institutions. Their children were also regarded unfavorably.

The CCP's policy of "integration and control" of overseas Chinese was very pragmatic. During the economic crisis following the Great Leap Forward, the CCP invented the "Foreign Remittance Certificate" in order to increase its foreign currency reserve to buy sophisticated products and technologies, including military ones. Any returned overseas Chinese or relatives of overseas Chinese who received foreign remittances could exchange foreign currency for Foreign Remittance Certificates and use the latter in special supply stores to buy milk formula, sugar, expensive groceries, and meat products beyond their regular rations and goods unavailable in regular stores. By this means, the regime maximized foreign remittances.

I recall that an old classmate of my father's was a professor of physics who came back to China after studying in France. His younger sister lived in the US, and after learning about the economic distress in China, she and her husband sometimes remitted some money to him so that he could stay nourished. This friend of my father's was very kind, and since he knew my father was in poor health, he occasionally gave him some Foreign Remittance Certificates so that my father could also buy some much-needed nourishment. However, during the Cultural Revolution, this kind friend was denounced by the Red Guards as the imperialists' slave and was forced to sweep the grounds of the university campus. He attempted suicide several times.

Another man whom I knew very well had a master's degree in civil engineering from a US institution and his wife was a distinguished graduate of Jinling Women's College. In 1955, the couple returned to mainland China from the US. The husband was assigned to a teaching position at a technical college in Nanjing. Since his father had served as the KMT government's ambassador to foreign countries, he was labeled a "spy suspect" in his files. He was denounced in every political movement and was interrogated as to why he abandoned his lifestyle abroad and whether he had any secret agenda. He could only work as an entry-level teacher and never got any promotion. During the Cultural Revolution, he was effectively imprisoned for many years, and his wife and two young children were exiled to the most impoverished rural area in Northern Jiangsu Province to work as peasants. In 1980 the family moved back to the US. Many years later, I happened to meet them, and this retired engineer in his seventies said to me emotionally:

> *I have very seldom cried in my life. However, when I returned to the US after being away for 25 years, immediately after I got to the customs, a customs officer said to me kindly: "Sir, welcome to the United States!" I couldn't hold back the tears. I sincerely wanted to serve my motherland, but the communists took me for an enemy and I could no longer stay there. Instead a foreign country thousands of miles away welcomed me so warmly.*

United Front work involving returned overseas Chinese was normally handled by local governments' Overseas Chinese Divisions. The Overseas Chinese Affairs Office of the State Council managed affairs of overseas Chinese who resided in foreign countries jointly with the Ministry of Foreign Affairs and the Ministry of State Security. This latter function was coordinated by the CCP Central Committee's Foreign Affairs Office and local governments were not allowed to handle it directly. The CCP's main policy toward overseas Chinese was to cultivate pro-CCP overseas Chinese community leaders and enhance its international propaganda to compete with Taiwan's Overseas Chinese Commission in terms of political influence. But the implementation of this policy depended on the CCP's attitudes toward specific foreign countries. Also, the CCP regime has never recognized dual citizenship and doesn't consider protection of overseas Chinese to be its duty. When waves of anti-Chinese riots hit Southeast Asia, especially Indonesia, during the 1960s, the CCP regime paid lip service to the protection of Chinese immigrants but only rescued family members of those with connections to the CCP's intelligence agencies. The plight of large numbers of Chinese immigrants without high social standing were ignored and the riots ran their course, resulting in a huge loss of Chinese lives. Similarly, during the severe persecution of Chinese immigrants in Cambodia in the 1970s, the CCP supported the Khmer Rouge regime and paid little heed to the lives of Chinese immigrants.

Many overseas Chinese who fled Southeast Asia and returned to China in the 1950s and 1960s were automatically regarded as political outsiders and forced to endure a process of political sorting. Many low- to mid-status people were settled on Hainan Island to prepare land for agriculture. Hainan was an economic backwater at the time, and these people suffered greatly. Meanwhile, the CCP selected some pro-CCP students from families with good class background and sent them to high schools dedicated to returned overseas Chinese. Jiangsu Province opened such schools (including cram schools for new returnees) in Wuxi. These schools were managed by local overseas Chinese affairs offices.

At the time, returned overseas Chinese were concentrated in some provinces and municipalities on the coast, where the government's overseas Chinese affairs agencies organized Returned Overseas Chinese Associations (commonly called Overseas Associations) to facilitate their management. At the national level, there was an "All-China Returned Overseas Chinese Association," and its first president was Southeast Asia business titan Tan Kah Kee. The Overseas Associations were mass organizations in name only and subsidiaries of the Overseas Chinese Affairs agencies in reality. Their employee salaries and operational expenses were all funded by the government, and their cadres were ranked at various administrative levels. For example, full-time presidents, vice presidents, secretaries general were treated at deputy bureau level if they were PCC standing committee members and at deputy division level if regular PCC members.

Some cadres of the Overseas Chinese Affairs agencies were formerly underground CCP members from foreign countries, mainly Hong Kong or Macao. The manager of the Nanjing municipal Overseas Chinese Affairs Division's Secretariat Section returned to China from Hong Kong, where he had participated in the anti-Japanese guerrilla force as an underground CCP member. He had many overseas connections and knew that the CCP was very sensitive regarding overseas relationships, so he was very prudent and careful. He always handed over letters from overseas to the Party Organization for review. Sometimes his caution appeared somewhat excessive and the division's CCP branch secretary told him many times that correspondence with family members didn't have to be handed over. However, this manager never lowered his guard, and he lived in greater fear than when he was doing underground work overseas.

Another cadre who returned from Japan was the full-time secretary general of the municipal Overseas Association. He went to Japan at a young age to work as a barber and was severely discriminated against by the Japanese during WWII. As a result, he had a nationalistic hatred of Japan. After WWII, he opened his own barber shop and also became a member of the Japanese Communist Party. Later, after participating in pro-China demonstrations, he was monitored by Japanese police and his barber shop was vandalized by Japanese gangsters so many times that he was forced to give up the business. He returned to China in the mid-1950s. Since he was a Japanese Communist Party member and was also considered a patriotic overseas Chinese, he was given a job in the Overseas Association. As a full-time officer there, he was the organization's real leader. However, his many attempts to convert his Japanese Communist Party membership to CCP membership were unsuccessful and he remained outside the Party. He often complained that he had already withstood a test by joining the Japanese Communist Party, and it was unfair that he was denied CCP membership. He became a Rebel during the Cultural Revolution and accused the UFWD of carrying out a "bourgeois reactionary line" to deny his CCP membership application. It wasn't long before he was labeled a "spy suspect" during the "Purging Class Ranks Movement" and arbitrarily denounced. After the Cultural Revolution, his case was redressed, and he became a cadre once again. After all these hardships, he became convinced that mainland China was not a good place to live and he immigrated with his family to Japan again, where he resumed his old trade and regained Japanese citizenship. Because of the CCP's extremely nationalistic teachings, Japan was a country of devils in the eyes of most Chinese, even apart from the Japanese military's war crimes in China. However, even such an enemy state would never endlessly examine and discriminate against a naturalized citizen, and an immigrant could live and work in peace there.

Before the economic reform, the CCP regime conducted extremely strict political examinations of returned overseas Chinese. All vital state institutions such as public safety, the judiciary or the military could never recruit anyone with an overseas relationship. Cadres of these organs would immediately be examined as spy suspects if they were found to have relatives overseas or to have corresponded with people overseas. This was a routine function of the UFWD's Cadre Examination Office. Some cadres were politically reviewed for decades without knowing it and could be turned down for promotion for years. The root cause of the trouble might be an overseas relationship which the cadre carelessly included in his background when applying for a job.

This situation changed dramatically after the economic reform began. People who wanted to send their children abroad tried their best to seek out overseas relationships. A friend of mine who taught at a university couldn't become an associate professor because he was a returned overseas Chinese, but for this same reason he became a candidate for United Front work after the Reform. He rose to become a leader of the All-China Returned Overseas Chinese Association and the China Zhi Gong Party, and eventually a vice chairperson of the national PCC with benefits at vice premier level. Of course, the focus of overseas Chinese affairs had shifted from political monitoring to seeking investment. The CCP's self-contradictions can be seen at annual international propaganda conferences and overseas Chinese affairs conferences. Party Central officials in charge of diplomacy and state security still insist on the so-called "fight against westernization, fight against splitting, and fight against infiltration." They still regard overseas Chinese as outside forces and are politically wary of overseas Chinese everywhere. They equate a pro-CCP stance as patriotism and try their best to carry out intelligence activities among overseas Chinese. Above is the Party Central's attitude toward overseas Chinese. At local levels, however, as long as overseas Chinese bring in investment, their political status in assured. Some officials actively collude with lawbreakers among overseas Chinese businesspeople for personal profit. Overall, investment from overseas Chinese has played a major role in China's economic development since the economic reform began and overseas Chinese will play an important role in China's democratization.

Chapter 16: "Class Struggles" Inside the UFWD

On the surface, the CCP is a tightly organized and centralized political party. However, because of its class struggle ideology, intra-party factional struggles have existed from day one. Mao himself said: "There are parties outside the Party, and there are factions inside the Party. No parties outside the Party would be an imperial dictatorship, and no factions inside the Party would be strange indeed." However, the CCP has always referred to intra-party factional struggles as conflicts along political lines, i.e., the winners representing the correct line and the losers the wrong line. It is an innovation in CCP propaganda that the dark secrets of power struggles are hidden below "line conflicts."

Judging from the CCP's history, United Front work was originally the CCP's strategy in its political conflicts with the KMT. This strategy enabled the CCP to develop and expand during WWII, create fissures within the KMT during the Chinese Civil War, and incite defections of KMT military commanders. It achieved significant political victories and finally resulted in the CCP's takeover of mainland China. After the CCP regime was established in 1949, three cliques were formed unofficially. Competition between these cliques dominated mainland China's political developments for thirty years, from 1949 to 1979, when the economic reform began. This is clearly seen in the so-called class struggles and line struggles within United Front institutions.

The CCP Central Committee's first institution dedicated to United Front work was the Urban Work Department, established in Yan'an in 1944. At the time, it was in the charge of Liu Shaoqi, a member of the Secretariat, and its head was Peng Zhen. In 1948, it was renamed the UFWD and was headed by Li Weihan under Zhou Enlai's supervision. Its goal was to win over democratic figures in KMT-controlled areas and incite defection of KMT military commanders. After the establishment of the CCP regime, Mao Zedong was in charge of overall operations but was actually focused on the military, which he deemed to be his lifeline. All assignment of division-level cadres or above in the military had to be reviewed and approved by Mao. Without Mao's approval, not a single company of troops could be dispatched. The second-highest CCP leader, Liu

Shaoqi, was mainly in charge of the Organization Department, the Propaganda Department, and the Beijing municipal CCP committee. The "Gang of 81 Traitors," which the Red Guards exposed during the Cultural Revolution, were actually Liu-clique cadres. Zhou Enlai and Chen Yun were in charge of the United Front, the government, the judiciary, intelligence, and finance. The UFWD was nominally carrying out Mao's directives but in reality was Zhou's political domain. Liu Shaoqi attempted to meddle in UFWD affairs, but his trusted lieutenants Liu Ningyi and Liu Xiao had always been excluded from the power core of the United Front system ever since the Pan Hannian incident, in which Pan, a former intelligence chief, was arrested in 1955 and later sentenced to life in prison. Therefore, before the Cultural Revolution there were three informal cliques among CCP cadres: Mao's military clique, including his trusted comrades-in-arms Luo Ronghuan, Lin Biao, and Xu Shiyou, and a few provincial party bosses, including Ke Qingshi and Wang Renzhong; the Liu Shaoqi clique, which controlled the Party Central's organization, propaganda, and cultural and education institutions plus the Beijing municipal CCP committee; and the Zhou Enlai clique that controlled the State Council and the government, the United Front, and the treasury. Mao had always been an absentee boss in administrative affairs and never bothered with details, and he gradually became unfamiliar with the situations inside Liu and Zhou's cliques. After the CCP's Eighth National Congress, and especially after Peng Dehuai's Ten-Thousand-Word Letter at the Lushan Conference and the Conference of Seven Thousand Cadres after that, Mao felt in danger of becoming a figurehead, which contributed to his decision to initiate the Cultural Revolution.

Under these political circumstances, the UFWD became a battleground between Liu and Zhou. From the establishment of the regime until 1964, the central UFWD had always been headed by Li Weihan, a key member of Zhou's clique. Li and Zhou both attended a work-study program in France and were both leaders of the CCP Delegation in the KMT-CCP negotiations near the end of WWII. Li Weihan became the CCP's authority on United Front theory, chaired twelve of the thirteen National United Front Conferences before 1964, and personally drafted conference documents. In 1963, he published the theory of "Two Alliances of Classes," which argued that during China's socialist revolution and construction, the United Front consisted of a primary alliance between the working class and the peasant class, and a secondary alliance between the primary alliance and the bourgeoisie and intellectuals. Nine of the national United Front conferences before the Cultural Revolution were directed or attended by Zhou Enlai, and others were directed or attended by Deng Xiaoping and Peng Zhen. Zhou was very familiar with the reality of United Front work and paid more attention to the adjustment of relationships between the Party and non-CCP democratic figures and intellectuals. In 1962, he even dispatched Chen Yi to attend the Intellectual Work Conference in Guangzhou and speak about "removing labels and bestowing crowns." However, these maneuvers by Zhou and Li were not approved of by Mao. Ever since the Anti-Rightist Campaign, because of leftist sentiment and apparent paranoia regarding minor political parties, Mao often behaved inconsistently, sometimes calling for adjusting relationships and other times stressing the importance of class struggle, which left the UFWD at a loss for what to do. As one democratic figure said privately, the CCP's United Front policy was like a baker kneading dough, sometimes slapping and sometimes stretching. This description illustrates the genius of Mao's United Front work.

In reality, the so-called line struggles within the Party reflected factional fights for political control. All factional conflicts were disguised as line struggles in the name of the bolshevization of the Party.

During the early stages of WWII, Wang Ming and Zhou Enlai fought for control over the leadership of United Front work. In the end, Zhou with his skillful political maneuvers and with the help of Mao and Liu drove Wang Ming out of the leadership and labeled him a right-leaning surrenderist. After the establishment of the CCP regime, Zhou Enlai always considered United Front work to be within his domain and prided himself on being the Party's authority on United Front work. He served as the chairperson of the national PCC from 1954 till his death in 1976. Zhou never loosened his control over United Front work and personally arranged for his trusted aide Li Weihan to be the head of the central UFWD. After the CCP's Eighth National Congress in 1956, Liu Shaoqi, as Mao's appointed successor, attempted to exert overall control of the Party. Liu arranged for Xu Bing to serve as the administrative vice head of the central UFWD and for Peng Zhen to be in charge of United Front work in the central secretariat. The so-called "81 Traitors" exposed during the Cultural Revolution were actually high-level cadres of the CCP's former underground Northern Bureau led by Liu. Therefore, there were two cliques in the UFWD, one from the military intelligence system and the other from the underground CCP system, each with its behind-the-scenes supporter. The two cliques took advantage of the so-called new trends in class struggles to oppose each other both openly and covertly.

The first wave of conflict occurred at the time of the Anti-Rightist Campaign of 1957. Although the main targets of this campaign were non-CCP democratic figures and intellectuals, some intellectuals inside the Party were also pursued because of their dissenting opinions about factionalism of the Party. High-level officials who were affected included the governor of Zhejiang Province, Sha Wenhan, and the director general of the provincial Organization Department, Chen Xiuliang, both of whom were formerly important leaders of the underground CCP and led United Front work for a while before the campaign. Additional conflicts occurred during the Anti-Right-Leaning Movement after the Lushan Conference, which affected both central and provincial UFWD's. The vice head of the central UFWD, Liu Geping, was one of the key members of the underground Northern Bureau but didn't belong to the "81 Traitors" because he never signed any written repentance while in KMT prison. He was universally disliked, persecuted during this wave of conflicts, and demoted to the position of deputy manager of a factory in Shanxi Province.

During this period of conflict, former underground CCP members who had no patrons were often denounced and persecuted because of their personal relationships or experiences. For example, a division director and a section-level officer of the Nanjing municipal UFWD faced such persecution. Although they didn't lose their jobs, they worked under surveillance while being investigated. However, cadres from the military intelligence system and those from the underground CCP system with Zhou Enlai were spared.

In April 1962, the twelfth United Front Work Conference was held, where the policy of "adjust relationships and mobilize positive factors" was announced. This alleviated the tense political atmosphere in sync with the national economic policy "adjust, solidify, augment, and elevate." However, less than half a year later,

Mao reversed course at the Beidaihe Conference and the Tenth Plenary Session of the Eighth Central Committee, demanding that the Party "never forget class struggles" and "discuss class struggles every day, every month, and every year." To adapt to this new trend in class struggle emphasized by Mao, the Socialism Education Movement (the so-called "Four Cleanups") was implemented in rural areas. Liu Shaoqi sent his wife, Wang Guangmei, to a rural village to develop the "Taoyuan Experience" in an apparent attempt to gain control of the movement. Meanwhile, a new anti-right-leaning campaign was carried out inside the Party. Liu-clique United Front cadres launched an attack on Zhou-clique cadres, resulting in Li Weihan, head of the central UFWD for almost fifteen years, being denounced. In April 1963, the central UFWD held a department affair meeting, at which a delegate from Party Central made a summary speech saying that the central UFWD had held thirty-five meetings but had never grasped the core of the problem, i.e., the UFWD didn't have a clear understanding of the issue of class. In May 1964, the Party Central held a working meeting, where Mao posed the question, "Is it possible for revisionism to emerge in China?" According to Mao:

> *The UFWD is supposed to deal with domestic bourgeoisie, but some of its members never talk about class struggle....Aiming to convert bourgeoisie political parties to proletariat ones and even making a 5-year plan for that purpose is to surrender to the bourgeoisie.*

In August, following Mao's address, the central UFWD held a department affair meeting to initiate the second round of denunciations of Li Weihan. In December, the department submitted Central UFWD's Report on Problems of Comrade Li Weihan to the Party Central, in which eight charges against Li were listed. On December 25, the Party Central decided to remove Li Weihan from the position of department head. He was also dismissed from his position as vice chairperson and standing committee member of the national People's Congress. Denunciation of Li was communicated to lower levels in a Party Central document which implicated several cadres. Many were excessively criticized and lost their positions for no wrongdoing. This became the preamble of the Cultural Revolution in the United Front system.

As Liu Shaoqi was denounced during the Cultural Revolution, the UFWD's internal "class struggles" implicated many cadres from the former underground CCP system, all of whom, with very few exceptions, became targets of examination and denunciation.

Chapter 17: Leaving the UFWD in Handcuffs

Shortly after National Day in 1965, I was sent by the UFWD to a university in suburban Nanjing to participate in the training of the second working corps of "Grassroots Socialism Education," organized by the Nanjing municipal CCP committee. Over two thousand cadres (mostly CCP members) from provincial and municipal institutions, schools, and enterprises participated in the training. The leader was Gao Liguang, deputy secretary of the municipal CCP committee, and the deputy leader was vice mayor Chen Shenyan. The training included studying the Party Central's documents about the Socialism Education Movement, listening to an audio report about Wang Guangmei's "Taoyuan Experience" as a model of the "Four Cleanups Movement" in rural areas, and speeches of municipal CCP leaders Peng Chong and Liu Zhong. Trainees were divided into several sub-corps: the first was slated for socialist education in state-owned large enterprises, the second for small and medium-sized local enterprises, and the third for township and village administrations. I was assigned to the second sub-corps and served as the deputy leader of a small team. The team leader was Tao Jian from the Urban Development Bureau, and along with four young cadres of this bureau we constituted a team to work in enterprises under the Second Industry and Transportation Department. After New Year 1966, I led a working group consisting of myself and two team members to establish a presence in a large collectively-owned factory administrated by the municipal Ceramics Company.

Immediately after entering this factory, we separately visited many shops and offices to learn about the Socialism Education Movement that had already begun under factory CCP committee leadership. We learned that the factory CCP committee had already labeled seven or eight people as members of a "reactionary ring." The alleged ringleader was a veteran who had worked in this factory since its founding. After deeper investigation, we realized that these senior workers only had complaints about the work style of factory leaders and the chaotic management of factory finances. For these reasons alone, they were considered troublemakers by factory leadership. The "ringleader" elaborated on his complaints about factory leaders' privileges and their using factory resources for personal purposes. Our group deliberated and concluded that the factory CCP committee had erred in directing the spearhead of socialism education toward the denunciation of workers. After we reported the situation to the leadership of the sub-corps, they asked us to further investigate in order to develop a detailed plan of socialism education.

In April, the sub-corps notified us of a collective study of the Party Central's editorials denouncing the opera *Hai Rui Dismissed from Office*. We all felt a political storm was looming. Soon, the Central Cultural Revolution Group was formed, and Party cadres collectively studied the May 16 Notification. Around this time, Red Guards went onto streets to destroy the "Four Olds," and there were scenes of "red oceans" with everyone waving a copy of the Little Red Book. Some workers in the factory planned to form Rebel organizations.

At the end of June, I was suddenly ordered to take along my group members to join Tao Jian in his investigation at the municipal Pedicab Company. A few days after we had established a presence there, the Red Rebel Command Center was formed. Mr. Wang from the Xiaguan Pedicab brigade became its commander, leading over two thousand drivers to hold a power-seizing assembly in the sports field of the Fifth Municipal Middle School. They seized the vice secretary of the municipal CCP committee, Mr. Wang, the director general of the Second Industry and Transportation Department, and the director general of the Urban Development Bureau, and brought them to the assembly to be denounced. Tao Jian and I went along to accompany targets of denunciation and stood in a row with the principal targets. The purpose of the denunciation was to expose capital roaders who carried out the reactionary line of the bourgeoisie. We were told to surrender the black materials we allegedly collected to persecute the Rebels. The denunciation lasted the whole day and almost the whole night, and we were forced to assume the so-called "jet posture" the whole time. Red Guards from Nanjing University and the Municipal Fifth Middle School also came to cheer on the Rebels. When the denunciation ended after 3 am the next morning, the denouncers and the denounced were all exhausted. The chairperson of the assembly announced that all these capitalist roaders would be taken to the Pedicab Company for detention and examination. We were thrown into two offices on the second floor of the Pedicab Company building, and the Rebels provided some comforters and mats for us to sleep on the floor. This was the first time I rested together with high-level officials such as the vice secretary of the municipal CCP committee, who joked that this was like his guerrilla warfare days in northern Jiangsu Province during WWII, when he was forced to sleep on the floor.

A few hours later, the Rebels delivered deep-fried breadsticks, steamed stuffed buns, and soy milk, and we had an excellent breakfast. Later they ordered us lunch containing meat and vegetables from a restaurant. In the afternoon, we were paraded through the streets. Each of us was forced to wear a tall hat made of paper, hold a worn-out gong, and display a paper banner on our chests. A big banner of the Pedicab Rebel Command Center was carried in the front of the parade. While marching, the Rebels shouted slogans through loudspeakers and beat gongs and drums, as if at a wedding procession. Over ten cadres wearing tall hats walked among the parade dispiritedly, beating gongs and shouting, "Defeat the reactionary line of the bourgeoisie!" "Revolution is not a crime!" and "Rebellion is justified!" Some Red Guards also participated in the parade. We circled the city center square and then marched to Changjiang Road Elementary School, where a short denunciation assembly was held. Afterwards, the Rebels escorted us back to the Pedicab Company for detention. After that, big and small denunciation assemblies were held against us every day for over a week.

After nearly ten days, several Rebels from the Ceramics Company wearing red armbands came to the Pedicab Company, negotiated with Commander Wang of the Rebels, and reached an agreement that I should be taken to the Ceramics Company. The leader of the visitors told me mysteriously, "We have gone to the provincial and municipal CCP committees to revolt and demand that you should be sent to our factory to solve the issue of the reactionary line of the bourgeoisie. Workers in our factory all assume that you are not on the side of the capitalist roaders and are protective of us workers." I couldn't decide whether I should laugh or cry. I said, "I have been denounced as an accomplice of the capitalist roaders in the Pedicab Company, while at the same time I have become a representative of the correct line in your company. I really don't know what I am." He said, "In any case, we are here to rescue you. Commander Wang has agreed that we should take you to our

166

company. He said Rebels should support each other. Please come with us." I asked Vice Secretary Wang whether I should go, and he answered, "Chairman Mao called on cadres to immerse themselves in mass movements to see the world and gain experience. Now that the masses there want you, you should go bravely." I took a pedicab to the ceramics factory.

The situation in the factory at this time was very chaotic, and production was at half capacity. Some office cadres and older workers formed a Workers' Battalion in opposition to the Rebels. Both factions wanted my support, putting me in a difficult spot. In the assembly to expose bad deeds, I tried to smooth things over by saying that I was a cadre who carried out specific tasks and was not among those in power, and that I was sent by higher authorities to this factory to conduct an investigation and hadn't figured things out when I was reassigned to the Pedicab Company. Personally, I considered the factory's management problems to be conflicts among people and not between classes. I hoped workers could maintain solidarity and implement the revolution while improving production, etc. In the end, neither faction was happy with what I said, and I was disliked by both sides.

Around this time, the municipality had fallen into social disorder. Bands of Red Guards went everywhere to destroy "Four Olds" and get rid of "Cow Demons and Snake Spirits," and every day capitalist roaders were paraded on the streets. Suddenly a series of tragedies took place. The director general of the Education Department, Wu Tianshi, and his wife died during a street parade and denunciation. The dean of the Nanjing Psychiatric Hospital, Wang Weizeng, committed suicide, as did the renowned Yue opera actress Zhu Shuizhao. Soon afterward, Professor Qian Fengzhang of the Nanjing College of Technology, one of my dad's classmates at Southeastern University and an expert in radar, jumped from a building and killed himself. I personally witnessed the Red Guards beating to death the head nurse of the municipal Chinese Hospital, who was a Christian, because she refused to renounce God. When asked to choose between Jesus and Chairman Mao, she answered that both were good men, so the Red Guards beat her to death using leather belts. She was denounced and beaten from dawn to dusk and no one dared to defend her. An angel who had worked to save lives died miserably on the front steps of her hospital. To this day, every time I see the cross above a church, I can't help thinking of this kindhearted Christian martyr.

In early September, all working group cadres were directed by the military administration to return to their former work units to participate in denunciations, criticisms, and transformations. I reported back to the UFWD, where the entrance was closed to the public and every cadre was at a loss what to think or do. The regular functions of the UFWD could not be carried out. Rebel organizations had also formed in some organizations reporting to the UFWD, such as the Overseas Association, where a Red Rebel Corps of Overseas Chinese was formed, mainly consisting of students of the cram school for returned overseas Chinese. Among minor political parties and organizations, there were a Rebel Team formed by cadres of the Federation of Industry and Commerce and a Youth Rebel Team formed by cadres of the Christian Youth Association. They sought the support of college students and kept attacking the UFWD, demanding that UFWD leaders surrender their seals so that the Rebels could seize power.

At the time, the UFWD's administrative deputy director general was hospitalized, and only the deputy director general in charge of ethnic and religious affairs and the director of the department office were there to carry on department business. To cope with attacks on the department's office compound by external Rebel organizations, all cadres and workers of the UFWD agreed to form an internal Rebel organization of our own to "seize power" nominally and confront and repel external Rebels. Overnight, all cadres below division level became members of the Rebel organization. We claimed to denounce the two remaining department leaders as power holders and used this as an excuse to secure classified materials.

The Rebels of the Overseas Association gathered together over a hundred people, including some Red Guards from high schools, and came to the UFWD to seize power and denounce Director General Wang, who had already been detained for weeks and denounced by Red Guards of the Nanjing Telecommunication School. Young cadres debated with them and claimed that since internal Rebels had already seized power of the UFWD, external forces were powerless. The two sides quarreled and fighting nearly broke out. We secretly arranged for a cadre whose spouse was a military officer to go to the military to seek help. Several soldiers came and announced the military administration's order that Party and government institutions should not be attacked. This ploy was effective because the Rebels were afraid of soldiers in uniform. Everyone was exhausted and the Rebels finally retreated.

Soon, the whole city erupted into a state of conflict. Depending on their attitudes toward the military administration, Rebels in Nanjing belonged to one of two factions: the "Red Headquarters" or "August 27." They marched on the streets and confronted each other every day. Later, an incident occurred at the Nanjing Automobile Factory when six or seven workers died, raising tensions in the city.

Under these chaotic circumstances, UFWD cadres had nothing to do but to briefly touch base in the office every day, read newspapers, chat in small groups of two or three people on all kinds of topics from political hearsays to trivial life affairs, and then go onto the streets to watch the demonstrations. This lasted until March 1968, when the provincial Revolutionary Committee was formed and Xu Shiyou became its chairperson, issuing an order that all cadres must return to their work units to carry out revolutionary activities. Cadres were organized to study "Six Provisions on Public Safety" and to denounce "Cow Demons and Snake Spirits" in their work units in the name of "cleaning the class team." The first victims were those with rightist labels and those who had questionable histories.

Inside the municipal UFWD, there were intense factional struggles resulting from conflicts in the provincial UFWD, where the director general, Mr. Gao, publicly supported the "August 27" faction and retreated with it to northern Jiangsu Province. The other faction came up with the slogan "Uncover the Mastermind of Crimes." It seemed every cadre in the provincial UFWD identified with one of the two sides, either pro-Gao or anti-Gao. In the Nanjing municipal UFWD, the director general and his deputies took different sides. The two factions held separate study sessions and meetings.

As for democratic figures in the PCC, minor political figures, and the Federation of Industry and Commerce, they were like members of enemy classes doing supervised labor, going to offices on time every day to tidy up, read newspapers, and study *Selected Works of Mao Zedong*. Probably none of them avoided denunciation by Red Guards, and many were beaten. For example, when Red Guards started sweeping away Cow Demons and Snake Spirits, many high school Red Guards carrying military belts stormed into the Federation of Industry and Commerce and interrogated everyone present. Anyone who admitted to be a capitalist was whipped with belts and forced to kneel and beg forgiveness. When the wealthiest capitalist, Mr. Liu, was interrogated, he only murmured that he had done business previously. No one else said anything, and the Red Guards thought he was a small business owner. They let him step to the side and he escaped through the back door. When the Red Guards came to Mr. Xu, who was obese and wearing nice clothes, they immediately concluded he was an arch-capitalist, beat him hard using belts, forced him to kneel, and denounced him for three hours. Later, UFWD cadres all laughed about this incident and praised Mr. Liu for being not only a shrewd businessman but also a master escape artist. Soon afterwards, the military administration sent officers to escort Mr. Liu to the Eastern China Hospital in Shanghai, where he was to receive medical treatment.

Around this time, the Rebels dispatched former PCC liaison officer Mr. Huang to represent the UFWD for managing United Front work targets in minor political parties. He assumed the title Commander Huang and behaved very pretentiously. He previously had to serve tea and hot water to minor political party leaders and clean up their offices, and now that he became their boss he was so proud that he lost his senses. He arrogantly called these people by their first names and directed them to serve hot water and sweep the floor.

Probably due to bad karma, after Mr. Huang had enjoyed his commander status for a few months, he was severely persecuted by the self-proclaimed Mao loyalist "Monk Commander" (i.e., Xu Shiyou, who was a monk before joining the CCP) during the Campaign to Ferret Out May Sixteenth Elements in 1970. He very nearly lost his life and was finally sent back to his hometown to work as a peasant. I don't know if his case was redressed after the Cultural Revolution. It seems that very few of the commanders at the time of the Cultural Revolution came to a good end.

In July 1968, an unforeseeable incident occurred, which became a turning point in my life. Since I lived in a one-story building, to guard against theft I put some valuable items into a suitcase and temporarily stored it in an old classmate's apartment, which I considered safer because it was located on an upper floor of a multiple-story building and the classmate's wife was a homemaker

170

staying home most of the day. However, this classmate was falsely accused of listening to enemy broadcasts and his apartment was searched. My suitcase was forcibly opened. They found several used notebooks inside, and Chairman Mao's portrait on the flyleaf of one of them was marked with a few red and blue circles. It was because a neighbor's boy had grabbed some of my colored pencils and scribbled on Mao's portrait. Two circles around Mao's eyes looked like a pair of glasses. I didn't pay much attention and saved this notebook along with others I had since it contained the contact information of some of my classmates. I could never have foreseen the consequences of not throwing this notebook away.

On the Friday after that, I sensed a strange atmosphere when I got to my office. A coworker immediately ran out and brought in two cadres who I didn't know, who said they were taking me to the former Personnel Division's office to discuss some issues. When I got there, they told me that I would be examined in isolation. I was detained in an empty room in the office building, guarded around the clock, and not allowed to go home. After what seemed like endless interrogations and denunciations, I gradually realized that the portrait of Chairman Mao on that notebook was the source of all the trouble. Despite my repeated explanations, the interrogators always believed I was trying to bluff my way out and insisted that I must admit I committed a counterrevolutionary crime opposing Chairman Mao. I was tortured for two weeks.

Finally, two people in military uniforms who looked like police officers participated in the interrogation for a few hours and then left. The next morning, a denunciation assembly consisting of all cadres of the United Front system was held with a banner reading "Bring Down Acting Counterrevolutionary Cheng Ganyuan." I thought I would surely be imprisoned, because this procedure was usually for arresting or executing prisoners after denunciation. So-called revolutionary cadres went to the podium one by one to expose and denounce me. To my surprise, two close friends of mine were among them. They accused me of having smeared the Cultural Revolution and Chairman Mao. They disclosed private conversations in which I supposedly expressed my failure to understand the demise of state president Liu Shaoqi, who was Mao's comrade-in-arms but was labeled a traitor and an enemy agent overnight. They also disclosed that I told them I had listened to the classified report of the Lushan Conference, in which Yang Shangkun claimed that Peng Dehuai said that Mao read too many ancient books and acted like a dynastic emperor who arbitrarily slaughtered ministers and generals. I realized that my so-called friends probably wanted to draw a clear line separating me from them, but how could they be so traitorous as to send me to the guillotine! I also recall that a female typist who had been very nice to me and joked in front of other people that "this is my little brother" surprised me by displaying extreme wrath and shouting, "We must knock this counterrevolutionary to the ground and step on him," as if she felt a deep animosity toward me. Also, a female colleague who worked in the same office came to the podium to accuse me of originating from a bureaucratic bourgeoisie family and of consistently opposing the Party and Chairman Mao. I figured that this colleague of mine had harbored hard feelings toward me after she learned I was sent by the department to do an external investigation of her history of cohabiting with a KMT military officer before she joined the CCP.

The denunciation assembly lasted over three hours. It was clearly a case of "kicking a man when he is down." Without any reason to hate me, they saw this as an opportunity to score political points while completely destroying my career.

The assembly ended with the whole audience shouting, "Firmly crack down on the acting counterrevolutionary!" and "We demand the arrest and punishment of the acting counterrevolutionary!" Finally, a PLA officer came to the podium and announced the decision to have me immediately arrested. Two fully-armed soldiers handcuffed me and escorted me onto a small SUV outside the assembly. The siren roared and my head was pushed down by the soldiers so that I couldn't see outside. I was on my way to the Nanjing Detention House.

This detention center was built during the Japanese occupation to detain anti-Japanese fighters. After China's victory in WWII, the KMT used it to detain suspected CCP members. Now it was used by the CCP to detain counterrevolutionary political prisoners. It was located at Wawaqiao, which literally meant "children's bridge." The building had an east wing and a west wing, with the warden's office in the middle. Every detainee entering the facility was strictly searched. Detainees were referred to by number and not by name.

At the time, my cell held ten detainees. Apart from three thieves whose identities hadn't been determined, the other seven all seemed to be newly detained political prisoners who had committed "counterrevolutionary crimes." The charges against two of them were ludicrous. One was an almost illiterate worker in his twenties who operated the boiler in a factory. Because of the Cultural Revolution, the factory stopped production, and several workers of the boiler shop gathered together to drink and chat. As they became intoxicated, they started to talk about women. One guy said that old men still liked young women and another guy claimed that old men were unable to enjoy sex with a young woman. This guy allegedly made fun of Chairman Mao, saying, "Chairman Mao is much older than Jiang Qing, which proves he likes young women!" He was immediately warned not to utter nonsense. However, less than ten days later, the factory held an assembly to study and implement "Six Provisions on Public Safety," and attendees were asked to expose acting counter-revolutionaries. This man was grabbed from the audience and pulled onto the stage, where he was whipped by Red Guards using belts. He was then handcuffed and sent to the detention house.

Another detainee was a 14-year-old boy from the countryside. He appeared to be very childish and naïve and was from a rich peasant family. When he was working the land, he suddenly needed to defecate. He did it in the field and used a piece of newspaper he found nearby to wipe his ass. However, in doing so he smeared a picture of Chairman Mao with his feces. This was found out by other peasants and this honest boy became an acting counterrevolutionary. Without having experienced similar events, later generations will probably never be able to imagine that such absurdity actually took place in the 1960s. Because of his origin in a rich peasant family, this poor kid was sentenced to ten years in labor camp. He was from Jiangning County, but since I didn't get his address, I haven't been able to inquire into his current situation.

For a couple weeks after my arrival in the detention house, I was subjected to rush interrogations, usually in the form of fatigue interrogation at night. Since I didn't admit any guilt, I was corporally punished with kneeling and 90-degree bending. The interrogators were all PLA soldiers and officers from the military administration. One of them was an older officer, and probably because he sympathized with me after learning I was a Korean War veteran, the interrogations became less intense, and I was sometimes even offered cigarettes. Afterwards, no one showed any interest in my case.

Around 1969 Chinese New Year, the cult of Mao reached its climax. Every inmate was given a Little Red Book and had to stand in a row in the cell every morning and evening to read Mao's quotations aloud and then wish the Great Teacher, Great Leader, Great Commander, and Great Helmsman Mao Zedong a long life. The detention house instructed inmates' families to provide comforters but didn't allow visits. My mother sent me a comforter, an overcoat, some crackers, and a short letter. Food from outside was not allowed in the cells. However, the warden on duty at the time was Mr. Sun, formerly director of the detention house and demoted to warden after Rebels seized power in the beginning of the Cultural Revolution. Himself victim of the Cultural Revolution, he was sympathetic toward inmates who were former cadres. Therefore, when he handed the comforter and the overcoat to me, he took me to an interrogation room, took out the crackers from my mother, closed the door, and asked me to eat them there without telling anyone. Since there were too many crackers for me to finish, I hid the remainder in my pockets and took them back to share with my cellmates.

I was previously acquainted with one inmate named Mr. Qin from the First Division of the Public Safety Bureau. He was formerly a capable cadre of the CCP's underground intelligence system who had taken advantage of his uncle's being a colonel-rank director in the KMT government's Ministry of Defense to find a job in the ministry and serve as a captain-rank secretary. He furnished a lot of valuable intelligence to the CCP during the Chinese Civil War and hence was credited for meritorious service. However, he was detained soon after the Cultural Revolution started because he was suspected of being a KMT spy. Coincidentally, his uncle, as an historical counter-revolutionary who had received leniency and been employed as a worker in the vegetable market before the Cultural Revolution, was also detained for investigation at this time and was in my cell. In the beginning, he didn't talk to any of his cellmates. Much later, he overheard that I was from the municipal CCP committee and started to talk to me about himself. He said he was detained probably because of his nephew's case, and not until hearing this did I realize that Mr. Qin was jailed in the same detention house. Mr. Qin was released after the end of the Cultural Revolution in 1976 and later served as provincial procurator-general and vice chairperson of the provincial People's Congress. Another inmate who had been detained for a longer period was the former general manager of the Xiaguan Power Plant, Mr. Xie, who was labeled a Hu Feng clique member and had been detained since the Hu Feng case in 1956. Although there was no clear evidence, he was kept in detention until 1976.

Since I was not in the same cell as Mr. Qin, I could only see him when we were out of our cells for exercise, though we couldn't speak to each other. Once, I saw him from a distance, and it seemed he also saw me, so we nodded to each other. However, this trivial gesture was noticed by the warden, a woman who had retired from competitive sports and transferred to the public safety system. She handcuffed me behind my back and told me to confess that I was sending some sort of signal. The handcuffs were not removed until she concluded that I wasn't hiding anything.

I was detained until September 1969, for a total of one year and nine days. As written on the notice of release, the conclusion was I did smear the splendid image of the Great Leader Chairman Mao but would be returned to my original work unit for disciplinary action in lieu of criminal prosecution. At this time, the municipal UFWD and other regular institutions had ceased to exist, and all municipal cadres had been concentrated in the "May 7th Cadre School" in Jiangpu Farm, a former *laogai* camp, for the so-called denunciation, criticism, and transformation of cadres. I was sent from jail to the May 7th Cadre School directly, where it was announced that I was a target of the proletarian dictatorship, and I had to work and live together with *laogai* inmates who were "Cow Demons and Snake Spirits" in a state of isolated investigation. During this period, I did the heaviest work on the farm along with the so-called "capitalist roaders with historical problems" and targets of denunciation.

At first, I worked as a porter for a building construction project. My task was to transport bricks from a brick and tile factory nearly two miles away using a handcart. Over 500 bricks, weighting possibly a metric ton, had to be carried each trip, and porters worked in pairs, one holding the handles and the other dragging the rope. Each day, we worked nine hours and made seven or eight trips.

After the building was completed, I was given various tasks such as digging a fish pond, carrying river mud, and working the land, starting at sunrise and returning at sunset. I could withstand the physical fatigue because I was young and strong. What was harder to withstand were the repeated denunciations, which usually happened in the evenings. Afterwards I would go to bed and fall asleep immediately.

I spent 1970 Chinese New Year at home. It had been one and a half years since I disappeared and my kids had difficulty recognizing me. My mother told me that after I was arrested, Rebels came to my parents' home and put up a big banner on the door reading "Knock Down Acting Counterrevolutionary Cheng Ganyuan," which of course put intense pressure on my family, and my kids were given contemptuous looks when they went outside. My parents were nearly seventy and I was really an unfilial son who let them down.

Soon afterwards, the "Down to the Countryside Movement" was implemented in the whole municipality per directives from provincial Revolutionary Committee president Xu Shiyou. Educated youth were sent to rural areas to strengthen their faith in communism. Cadres were sent there to be reeducated by the peasants, in reality to exile to rural areas those cadres who were denounced in the Cultural Revolution or originated from a wrong class. Over 300,000 residents of the municipality were transported. In the May 7th Cadre School, cadres were asked to enlist in the Down to the Countryside Movement. In reality, regardless of whether you enlisted or not, the list was determined internally and those on the list had no way to escape.

A member of the working class propaganda team of the cadre school notified me that my case would be further processed. A CCP branch assembly was held, at which it was announced that my Party membership was stripped and that I was determined to be a class outsider who had sneaked into the Party. The reason for this strange label was that my father had served as director of the school inspector office of the bureau of education during the KMT era, making him a bureaucrat of the KMT regime and me the offspring of a reactionary bureaucrat. Actually, as a lifelong educator, my father only served as a normal school president and director of school inspection for less than four years. I argued vehemently with leaders of the Party branch, who were Rebels, and a few Party members couldn't tolerate the injustice and stood up to protest and argue on my behalf. Finally, the resolution to strip my Party membership was passed by a thin margin, and it was decided that my salary would be reduced by three ranks from Rank 20 to Rank 23 and that I would be sent to a rural village to work under supervision.

I was exiled to a rural village in northern Jiangsu in December 1970, and my five years there enabled me to truly experience the miserable existence of Chinese peasants. I lived and worked in a village of over thirty families, which was referred to as a "production team" in the People's Commune system. Only two families had members serving as cadres elsewhere: one of them worked at the supply and marketing cooperative and the other at an agricultural machinery factory. These two families were the only ones that lived in brick-and-tile dwellings; everyone else lived in adobe huts with earthen walls and thatch roofs. Many were so poor as to have no decent furniture. Some had only one cotton-padded comforter for five or six family members. The township arranged for me and another cadre—both of us without family members—to live in an adobe hut belonging to the production team beside its wheat threshing ground. The simple building had holes and cracks in all directions, and we temporarily used reed mats to reinforce the walls. In the winter, bone-chilling wind penetrated the walls and we had to sleep without taking off our clothes and were often woken up because of the cold. When this happened, I always recalled the ancient poet Du Fu's poem "Thatched Cottage Blown Open by Autumn Wind." Surely Mr. Du's situation at the time was not direr than mine.

What was more troublesome was that shortly after I was exiled to northern Jiangsu, my parents were told to move back to their hometown in Jixi County, Anhui Province. At the time, my father was seventy and my mother sixty-nine. They were still taking care of my second child, who was three. How could they survive in a rural backwater without electricity or running water? It would be very difficult for people my parents' age to haul well water. My mother was very stubborn and believed that there would always be a way out. Fortunately, a cousin of mine agreed to take care of my parents. I took a leave of absence from the village in northern Jiangsu and accompanied my parents back to our hometown in Anhui.

Every winter, hydraulic projects using the method of large legion warfare were carried out in northern Jiangsu Province with tens of thousands of laborers. The county set up a hydraulic construction militia corps and needed some educated people to do propaganda work like running broadcast stations at construction sites and editing and printing booklets and newsletters. I was chosen by the county revolutionary committee to do this almost every year, which was very advantageous. First, I could sleep in the construction sites' temporary sheds that had big stoves for heating. Second, I didn't have to do hard labor. Third, there was an extra stipend of 15 RMB a month when working on the construction sites, so I could remit a little more money to my parents and kids. The hydraulic projects usually lasted from October to March. At the time, a few recent college graduates and I were sent to the construction sites to set up and run a broadcast station and publish a printed newsletter called *Frontier of Controlling the Huai River*. I also became a correspondent of the provincial CCP newspaper on hydraulic projects. Usually, I was allowed to take a vacation for over a month after the end of each construction season so that I could go to my hometown in Anhui to see my family.

I witnessed the extreme poverty of peasants on the construction sites. Hydraulic laborers were mostly in the prime of their lives, and each production team dispatched between five and ten laborers. They lived in small shacks holding a handful of people, which were actually small pits on the ground about two feet deep padded with straw, containing a reed mat and covered with a teepee made of wooden sticks, reed mats, and straw mats for protection from wind and rain. The five or six laborers per shack would sleep naked and cuddle under one comforter to stay warm using their body warmth. During the coldest days, many laborers had only a pair of thin pants and a ragged cotton-padded jacket. (Some only had one ragged jacket without any other top wear and went topless in the summer). The extreme poverty of Chinese peasants was probably unique in the world and their living conditions were not much different from those of animals. Some old peasants told me that before the communist takeover, even though they were exploited by landlords, they always had enough food and warm clothes, and unless there was a big crop failure that prompted people to flee famine-stricken regions, usually no one starved to death. Seeing the dehumanizing situation of Chinese peasants under Mao's rule, I became completely disillusioned about the CCP's propaganda line, "Poor people are emancipated and become the master of their own affairs." I deeply felt that Mao cheated the world and used the blood and sacrifices of peasants to overturn the so-called "three big mountains" via communist revolution. It felt like I was waking up from a long dream and that Mao had broken all the promises he had made during the revolution and had reduced China to a society of serfs. Mao's Great Leap

Forward and the People's Commune Movement created extreme poverty in China's rural areas, worse than what existed during the ancient dynasties. Mao likened himself to Emperor Qin Shi Huang, but the cruelty of his rule went far beyond that of the Qin Dynasty.

After Deng Xiaoping reentered the CCP's leadership in 1974, some cadres denounced during the Cultural Revolution had their cases redressed. In September of that year, cadres from the Cadre Examination Office of the Organization Department of the Nanjing municipal CCP committee came to the county where I was exiled and notified me of the so-called "corrected conclusion." They announced their conclusion to me: I did commit a serious political mistake by smearing the portrait of Chairman Mao, but the punishment of dismissal from the Party was reduced to a two-year probation inside the Party, and my salary would be restored to 79 RMB per month. I firmly objected to this conclusion, quarreled with them for a whole day, and refused to sign it. Finally, I wrote "I completely disagree with the conclusion reached by the May 7th Cadre School" on a piece of paper and let them go back with it.

These several years were the lowest point of my life. During this time, I lost two members of my family. One of them was my second sister, Cheng Shufang. She was a very kind and honest woman who taught in a middle school after graduating from the Chinese Department of Nanjing Normal College. Highly introverted, she frequently had symptoms of depression. After witnessing students denouncing teachers during the Cultural Revolution, she was distraught and became schizophrenic. From the late 1960s to the early 1970s, she was admitted to psychiatric hospitals three times, the last being in 1972. After that, she was transferred to a psychiatric nursing home for long-term care. Due to the poor conditions there, she didn't receive medical treatment in time after a heart attack and died at the age of 38.

The other great loss was my father. He was a graduate of Southeastern University where he studied under Tao Xingzhi, and taught at the Education Department of Central University and that of Lantian Normal College in Hunan. After the victory in WWII, he returned to Nanjing and served as director of the school inspector office of the municipal bureau of education and president of the municipal normal school before returning to Central University as a professor and director of the registrar. Before the communist takeover, he disobeyed the underground-CCP-dominated School Contingency Committee's orders but followed the directive of Hu Jiajian, provost of the university, to secretly transfer over one thousand students' school records to Taiwan where they had fled, which enabled these students to complete their studies. The military administration of the school ordered my father to enroll in the Eastern China Revolutionary University's study group, where he should confess his history. My father refused to accept this arrangement and resigned from the university to become a literature and history teacher at the private Anhui High School (which became Municipal Sixth High School later) until his retirement in 1964.

Throughout his life, my father was an upright man who taught diligently and was loved by his students. In the 1950s, he became a delegate to the municipal People's Congress as a model teacher. Because of accusations made against me during the Cultural Revolution, he had to move back to his hometown with his family at the age of seventy. During his later years, he witnessed the persecution of intellectuals, the ravaging of China's education system, and the suicides of several good friends. As a result, he felt terrible grief and indignation. He told me privately that Mao's personal cult was in essence the same as Hitler's, and that Mao's end would not be any better than Stalin's. His downcast mood affected his health, and because healthcare in rural areas was so poor that seeing the doctor would require walking several miles to the county seat, he delayed seeking treatment until he became seriously ill. In February 1976, he was hospitalized in Ruijin Hospital, which was run by a third-front factory several miles from the county seat. Although the doctors were from Ruijin Hospital in Shanghai, the medical equipment was not good, and my father's illness became more and more serious. When I returned to my hometown after receiving a telegraph, my father had already been in hospital for over half a month. I stayed by his bed day and night. At the time, the hospital didn't provide any conveniences for family members, and I had to sleep on the floor beside my father's bed with my clothes on for a few hours each night. After over two months, I received a notice from the Organization Department of the county CCP committee ordering me to return to northern Jiangsu immediately to take care of the paperwork for my return to Nanjing. Since returning to the city was an important affair for all cadres living in exile, I had no choice but to rush to northern

Jiangsu. At the time, my first sister worked in Beijing and happened to be back in our hometown to visit my parents, so I asked her to stay with our father in the hospital. I stayed three days in northern Jiangsu to handle the procedure for transferring my files from the county to Nanjing. Shortly after 2 pm on the day after I reported to the Nanjing municipal Organization Department, I received an expedited telegraph from my mother saying that my father had passed away at noon.

On that day, I experienced a weird occurrence that I will never forget. At approximately noon, my daughter and I were in our apartment on the third floor of a residential building, and we both heard my father's voice calling me by my nickname twice, "Xiaojing, Xiaojing." We walked to the room off the hallway and opened the door. My daughter said she seemed to have heard Grandpa calling me. I said, "Yes, I also heard that." My heart was suddenly seized by an ominous premonition. Soon, the expedite telegraph arrived. I believe this was my father's last farewell to me from the world of spirits.

My pitiful father, you devoted your whole life to educating people. Intellectuals of your generation bore so much of the nation's burden. During WWII, you fled as a refugee to Hunan; in your later years, you became the victim of cruel political movements. My siblings and I never brought you much joy but caused you a great deal of trouble. I regret leaving your bedside before you left this world. If I hadn't hurried away to take care of the transfer procedure, you would probably have left the world with one less regret.

About a week after my father's funeral, I returned to Nanjing and stopped by the Organization Department to ask if my job placement had been completed. The answer was they hadn't found a work unit for me and that the UFWD hadn't been restored yet. There was only a working team reporting to the revolutionary committee, which meant it didn't need any more employees. Now that I was on personnel's blacklist of undesirables, I could do nothing but wait patiently.

One day, while walking on the street wearing a ragged military overcoat, I ran into a tall man in a military overcoat walking in the opposite direction, and we both stopped to look at each other. It turned out to be Mr. Wang, deputy director of the political department of an artillery division in the Korean War. He came up to shake hands with me and said, "You are Little Cheng! How come we ran into each other here." I knew that he was a deputy chairperson of the provincial science council before the Cultural Revolution, and that, because of his unyielding personality cultivated during his military service, he suffered immediately after the Cultural Revolution started. We shook hands firmly like long-time comrades-in-arms who had just come back from the battlefield. Seeing me in ragged clothes like a soldier of a defeated army, he asked where I had been exiled to during these years. I smiled and said I had worked as a peasant in northern Jiangsu. He said he was newly "liberated" and had just started working. We both laughed.

Mr. Wang then asked if I had found a new work unit, and I told him I had become an "undesirable." He wondered how a veteran of the Korean War could be persecuted to the extent of having nowhere to work. He then said straightforwardly: "I have just been assigned to the position of deputy director general at the Bureau of Geology and Mineral Resources. If you can't find a work unit, how about coming to my place and looking for minerals with me?" Sensing the intense spirit of a comrade-in-arms in Mr. Wang, I said, "Yes! How do I get started?" In this way, I finally found a work unit.

Soon after I started working in 1976, Mao died and the Cultural Revolution came to an end. I then went to the municipal CCP committee to file a complaint. I demanded further redress of my case and that I be compensated for five years of lost salary. Since my case involved Mao, the Cadre Examination Office of the municipal CCP committee dragged out my case without reaching any decision. In 1980, I went to the Central Organization Department in Beijing to seek help from the head of the Central Cadre Examination Bureau, Mr. Zhang, my former colleague in the Ministry of Interior. In 1959, I had been dispatched by the ministry to investigate his overseas relationships and never expected that he would one day review my own case. He agreed that my case was absurd and said that he would escalate it to Party Central leadership for directives. Not long after, CCP secretary general Hu Yaobang personally wrote a comment asking the Nanjing municipal committee to carefully reinvestigate my case. The Personnel Division of the restored Nanjing municipal UFWD changed the conclusion of my case to "having committed serious political mistakes, punished by serious warning within the Party, and all missed income should be made up." But why was it still "serious political mistakes," now that all mention of Chairman

182

Mao's portrait had been removed? I was told that the decision had been made by the municipal CCP committee and they just followed directives from above.

I had become completely disillusioned with the Party and didn't want to waste time on disputes over wording. I forced a smile and said, "My absurd political case can probably be written into the official history of the CCP as a rare spectacle in history."

The director asked if I had any requests concerning job placement. "Since you studied law, you can go back to the legal domain and can also return to the UFWD." I said I would think more about it. At this time, I worked as chief of the Employee Welfare Section of the Bureau of Geology and Mineral Resources. Director General Wang repeatedly urged me to stay, saying that the section would soon be elevated to division, and my position would rise. However, I had lost any interest in an official post in the CCP regime and finally chose to transfer to the Law Institute of the provincial Social Science Academy to do theoretical research on administrative law. From that point on, I embarked on an exploration of China's transition to a society of democracy and rule of law.

Chapter 18: Reflections on My Years in the UFWD

1

I belonged to the CCP's UFWD for nearly ten years, from my entry in 1961 to my exile in late 1970. I completely severed my ties with the UFWD in 1980, nearly 20 years after joining. These were the golden years of my life, when I was the strongest and most energetic. As Confucius said, "At thirty, I established myself. At forty, I was free from delusions." I joined the UFWD when I was over thirty. I worked extremely hard, wrote several million words of speeches, work reports, briefings, summaries, and correspondences, and was called a "writing machine" by friends and coworkers because I could finish a long draft of over ten thousand words in one night. My life had significant ups and downs: I went from being a model cadre of the Party to being a prisoner charged with active counter-revolutionary crimes; from being a cadre above the common people to doing hard labor in the field. It has been said that "suffering is the precious treasure of life." I must thank God for allowing me to pass through both heaven and hell and finally return to Earth with a positive, rational attitude.

During these years, I transitioned from being a zealot and loyal communist into being a rational explorer of constitutional democracy. I was like a traveler who has been trekking in the wrong direction and finally turns around to accompany the tide of history. Although I am tired, my heart is still filled with warmth and joy because the dark night is almost over and daylight is on the horizon. In some sense, if not for my experience with the Cultural Revolution, I might still be working mindlessly for the Party. For me, this is the silver lining of my experience.

2

My imprisonment from 1968 to 1969 prompted me to reflect on my past. I discovered the essence of the communist regime in China and the historical lessons of the Soviet Union. When the communist regime was established in China in 1949, I was a middle school student who resented the corruption of the KMT regime during its last years on the mainland and had great hopes for the CCP. I hoped that the nation would become rich and powerful and that our people would find happiness. Having been educated on communist propaganda, I became an enthusiastic admirer of Mao. In 1950, I answered Mao's calling to "guard our homes and defend our country" and enlisted on the wrong side of the Korean War. After that, I entered college with the intention of "building the motherland into a communist heaven." Despite the Anti-Rightist Campaign and the Great Leap Forward, I still considered myself a determined leftist communist who willingly served as the Party's "tame tool" with devotion to Mao. Not until the Cultural Revolution—when I experienced absurdities similar to Soviet generals shouting "long live Stalin" when they were executed during the purge—did I begin to question my own thinking.

Why do the communists cruelly slaughter their own comrades and even the common people? What was the origin of the cult of Mao and the Cultural Revolution?

I think the reasons are threefold:

The first is Marx's misleading theory of proletariat dictatorship. Marx held antisocial views. He envisioned the proletariat overthrowing the capitalist system via violent revolution and establishing a proletariat dictatorship. Errors were already detected in his activities and in the founding of the First Communist International. His slogan "Workers of the world, unite!" ignored the different conditions and different cultural and social development among nations. Marx was opposed by many political leaders of workers who participated in labor movements. Later, Lenin incited proletariat revolution in Russia and seized power from the so-called bourgeois democrats to establish communist rule. His successor, Stalin, took advantage of the despotic traditions of Russia to establish a personal dictatorship in the guise of socialism.

The CCP's path to power was different from that of the Russian communists but employed similar tactics. It incited peasant rebellions in the name of democracy, took advantage of the Japanese invasion to strengthen itself, and finally seized power from the KMT. Because of the paternalist tradition in Chinese culture, Mao easily established a one-party and one-man rule and became an emperor without a crown. To solidify his dictatorship, Mao pushed the theory of proletariat dictatorship to the extreme left and developed the theory of "continuous revolution under proletariat dictatorship," which resulted in domestic chaos and was the fundamental cause of the Cultural Revolution. The Khmer Rouge regime in Cambodia was the first testing ground of Maoism in foreign countries and the result was over two million deaths. Sihanouk claimed that the Khmer Rouge had turned Marxism into a religion. Mao's personal cult and his deification reached its peak during the Cultural Revolution.

After the calamity of the Cultural Revolution, the CCP leadership undoubtedly realized the absurdity of the theory of proletariat dictatorship. Deng Xiaoping abandoned the slogan of "continuous revolution under proletariat dictatorship" but didn't dare to confront Marxism's original errors for fear of weakening the foundation of his rule. We ended up with a form of crony capitalism under the banner of Marxism-Leninism.

Second, institutional flaws existed within the Party. Many CCP members who were denounced and persecuted during the Cultural Revolution had realized that the personal cult of Mao was a major problem. Deng said: "A bad institution can turn a good person into a bad one." The report of the CCP's 13th National Congress stated that the Party hadn't engaged in building democratic institutions after it seized power nationally and it attempted to achieve some breakthroughs in political reform. However, because of Deng Xiaoping's crackdown on the 1989 student movement, the 13th National Congress' resolution became useless.

Actually, although Mao used the slogan of actualizing democracy and ending the KMT's one-party rule to incite rebellions among the Chinese people when he was fighting the KMT regime, he was never a democratic-minded political leader. His political ideal was at the same level as that of peasant rebel leaders during the dynastic era who wanted to retain power forever. After the establishment of the CCP regime, everything Mao did was contradictory to the basic ideals of a modern rule-of-law society. He interrupted the development of a legal system in China, integrated the Party and the government, centralized power, made the court an administrative tool, and made all representative institutions rubber stamps. He had truly restored the despotic imperial institutions of ancient China.

Since its inception, the CCP has never been based on modern democratic principles, but has always operated according to the organizational norms of clans or mafias. In Mao and Deng's eras, the leader of the CCP acted very much like a mafia boss, possessing power over the military and the government as a dictator-for-life. Over the past twenty years, this irregular form of leadership has gradually been replaced by a system of regular replacement, i.e., with the leader stepping down at a certain age and the successor being hand-picked by the outgoing leader or even the previous one. This is a reincarnation of the ancient institution of abdication and far from a modern system of electoral competition.

Mao's crimes in the Cultural Revolution were not personal in nature, but the result of shortcomings in party institutions. Every CCP member who joined the Party before the Cultural Revolution should assume moral responsibility, and every central committee member should apologize sincerely to the people. Without this, they will never be able to face up to history.

Third, Mao's personal political character and personality must be considered. Mao entered the political stage as the leader of a peasant rebellion. He had extraordinary competence in political and military strategy. However, once he seized power, his outdated thinking going back to his peasant origins and his desire for power and personal gratification became apparent. He indulged in debauchery and continuously abused his power. As this grew, he became increasingly corrupt and depraved, and the negative side of his personality was fully exposed. He suffered from paranoia and viewed everyone with suspicion or hatred. Anyone who went against his will was considered an enemy and had to be eliminated. He took pleasure from persecuting his opponents to death. Mao had become an old man suffering from severe psychological illness. It is lamentable that this lunatic who is responsible for tens of millions of deaths is still enshrined on Tian'anmen Square as an object of worship. How can the Chinese people lead a normal spiritual life under such conditions?

3

As a political party work unit, the UFWD is an institution with "Chinese characteristics" that is not seen in any other political party in the world. However, its characteristics do not include a so-called cooperation of multiple parties. This is a false claim meant to deceive which the CCP continues to make to this day.

In fact, the United Front and the UFWD were established by the CCP as tools to collect intelligence and incite defection in the process of seizing power from the KMT regime. In fact, the UFWD could be considered an espionage agency working on the "fifth column." Throughout the CCP's struggles with the KMT, especially during WWII and the Chinese Civil War, the United Front was extensively utilized and deserves to be considered as one of Mao's "three magic weapons" responsible for the success of the Chinese communist revolution. Many prominent KMT figures—including Zhang Xueliang, Fu Zuoyi, Zhang Zhizhong, Cheng Qian, and Wei Lihuang —fell prey to the United Front. According to Mao, until Taiwan was united with the PRC and the KMT was neutralized, United Front work against KMT figures must continue.

After the CCP seized power in mainland China, Mao's strategy toward minor political parties and intellectual elites was to transform them into "tools of tools." Party members were the Party's tame tools, and minor political parties followed Party directives. Mao intended to turn the PCC and the minor political parties into the modern equivalent of the ancient Hanlin Academy, where intellectuals were kept on the payroll for use by the emperors. Mao approved of this ancient institution and sought out writers and poets such as Guo Moruo and Liu Yazi to chime with him.

Mao's actual practice was to gradually turn minor political parties into "intellectual ranches." His concept of "coexisting for the long term and monitoring each other" was meant to allow democratic figures to save some face. As one democratic figure put it, "We thank the Party for our long-term existence and don't dare to monitor the Party." After the economic reform began, some prominent figures of minor political parties discovered the CCP's true purpose in maintaining these parties and proposed to add the words "treat each other with total sincerity and share both honors and disgraces" to the CCP's United Front policy. This proposal vividly captured the essence of the United Front and was approved of by Deng Xiaoping. Actually, "treating each other with total sincerity and sharing both honors and disgraces" can only take place between close relatives and friends. The relationship between political parties should be equal and competitive. The CCP scolded the Communist Party of the Soviet Union for attempting to belittle the CCP as a "child party" and elevating itself as the "parent party," but what does the CCP do but belittle the minor political parties as "child parties"? It is shameless to claim that this political party system with Chinese characteristics is a superior one.

4

My purpose in writing this book is to expose the truth. Nowadays in China, it is not easy to speak the truth. Although parents often tell young children not to lie, everyone in China does so. In kindergarten, teachers pay special attention to those students whose parents make generous gifts. From elementary school to high school, those who report others to show their progressiveness are given priority in admission to the Young Pioneers and the CYL. In college, students learn to view people and the world through the lens of communist propaganda and behave submissively toward the powerful. Lies become the reality and truths become delusions. Some people's lives appear to consist of little more than lies.

Once a person reflects on his or her past with a deep feeling of reassessment and remorse, everything will become clear. In the Bible it is written: "I am sending you to them, open their eyes, and turn them from darkness to light, and from the power of Satan to God." (Acts 26:18)

Every time I see a large number of well-dressed people with briefcases entering the Roman-style assembly hall, raising their hands together, applauding together, and going to the podium one after another to read their speeches in a very deferential manner, I always recall the puppet shows that I used to participate in. I was the one pulling the strings behind the scenes under the supervision of the UFWD director general or the Party committee secretary. Every move of those puppets was controlled by string-pullers according to a pre-determined script.

Converting so many people into puppets without souls is a horrible corruption of human dignity. However, the dark side of humanity is often unable to resist the temptations of fame and wealth, and many people rush toward the abyss of evil like moths flying to a flame. Some legal research colleagues of mine often expressed discontent with the judicial system in China, but once they became PCC members or People's Congress delegates or were invited by UFWD leadership as distinguished guests, they changed dramatically, with some even attacking so-called heretical opinions. Once I came across a friend who had been listed among United Front work targets and was so pleased he nearly went out of his mind. He said, "I have finally obtained a high status." I said with a bitter smile, "Your files must have been transferred from your school to the UFWD, where your every word and action will be recorded. As long as you keep saying the right things, you will be rewarded politically and be able to enjoy the rest of your life. As for teaching and research, you no longer need to work hard, because you can use your political title to freeload and enjoy both fame and reward."

If a Party member willingly and self-consciously serves as a tame tool of the Party, we can't rule out the possibility that this is motivated by an obsession with Marxist ideology. However, those who enjoy serving as "a tool of a tool" are nothing but crass profiteers blinded by greed. The CCP nowadays is a corrupt band of bureaucrats riding roughshod over the people, and there is a consensus among Party members that the purpose of joining the Party is to obtain a political position. Despite the talk of "Three Representations," "Harmonious Society," and "Chinese Dream," the reality cannot be concealed. Under these circumstances, some intellectuals consider joining minor political parties as an alternative path to a political position, which is a reflection of the moral bankruptcy of Chinese intellectuals.

However, the tide of history cannot be reversed. The rise and fall of a society, a people, or a state is not determined by its level of economic development but by its institutions. This is an iron rule which no leader or political party can evade. When the Chinese intellectual wakes up from his political degeneracy and recognizes the global trend in social progress, when he stays clear of the trap of the United Front and refuses to serve as "a tool of a tool," and when the people consider it honorable to resist such an institution as the United Front, the Chinese nation will have cause to feel proud of itself.

This book is dedicated to those intellectual and business elites in mainland China, Hong Kong, Macao, Taiwan, and overseas who, at one time or another, have been targets of the CCP's United Front work. Let's pray that our sins will be pardoned and that we will emerge from darkness. May the Chinese people one day realize the dream of a constitutional democracy that is free, equal, just, and in accordance with the rule of law.

(The End)

Printed in Great Britain
by Amazon